Stories Carved in Stone

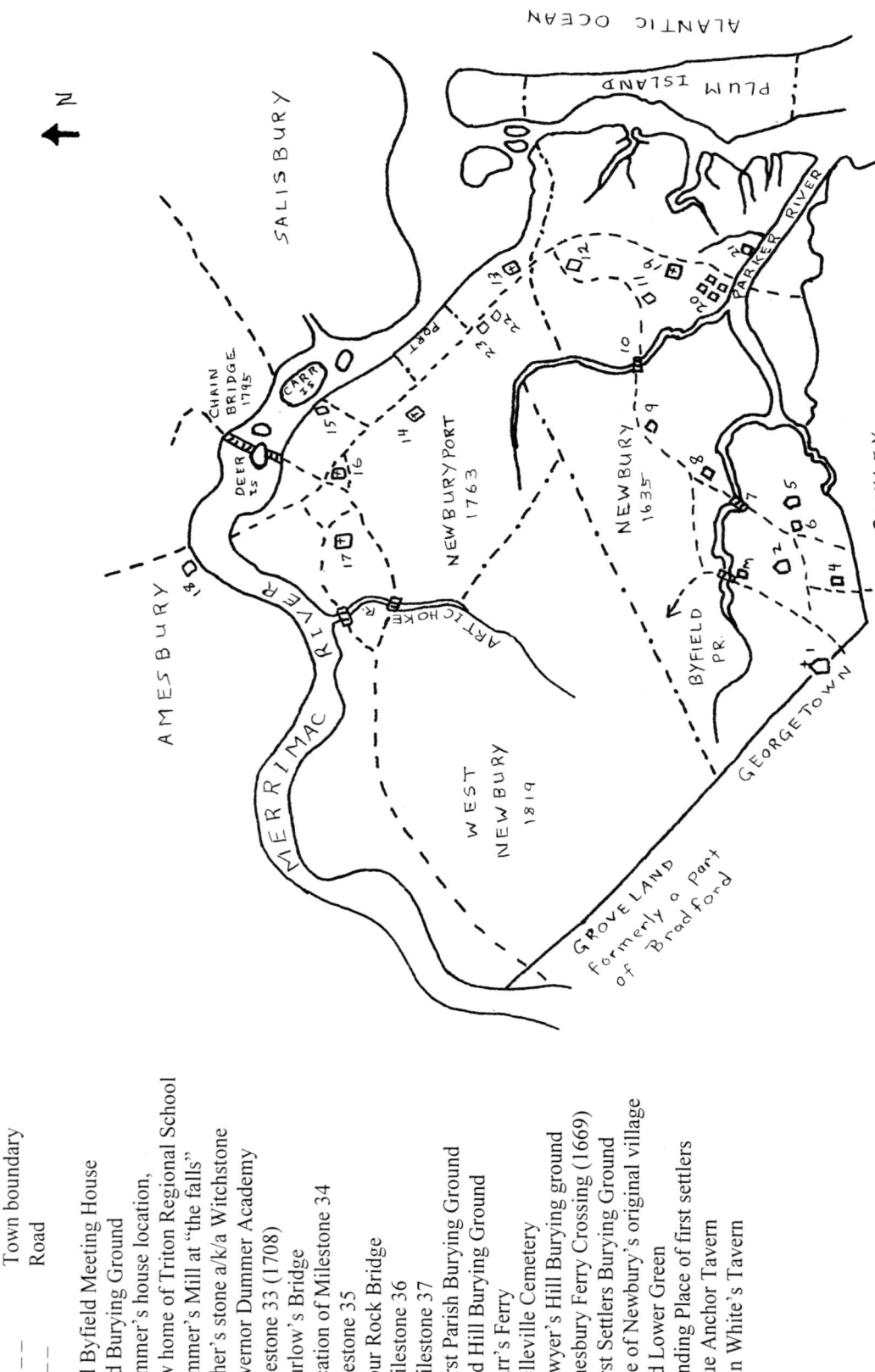

KEY

—··—··— Town boundary
————— Road

1. Old Byfield Meeting House and Burying Ground
2. Dummer's house location, now home of Triton Regional School
3. Dummer's Mill at "the falls"
4. Father's stone a/k/a Witchstone
5. Governor Dummer Academy
6. Milestone 33 (1708)
7. Thurlow's Bridge
8. Location of Milestone 34
9. Milestone 35
10. Four Rock Bridge
11. Milestone 36
12. Milestone 37
13. First Parish Burying Ground
14. Old Hill Burying Ground
15. Carr's Ferry
16. Belleville Cemetery
17. Sawyer's Hill Burying ground
18. Amesbury Ferry Crossing (1669)
19. First Settlers Burying Ground
20. Site of Newbury's original village and Lower Green
21. Landing Place of first settlers
22. Blue Anchor Tavern
23. Ann White's Tavern

Stories Carved in Stone

The Story of the Dummer Family,

the Merrimac Valley Gravestone Carvers,

and the Newbury Carved Stones,

1636-1735

Mary E. Gage
James E. Gage

☙ Powwow River Books ❧
Amesbury, MA
2003

Copyright © 2003, Mary E. Gage and James E. Gage. All Rights Reserved.

Except for brief quotation in articles or reviews, this book or parts thereof, must not be reproduced in any form or stored in any electronic format without written permission from the publisher.

Acknowledgements

Figures A, 2, 3, 8, 11, 45, 49, 50, 51, 56, 70 used with the permission of the Smithsonian Institute, National Museum of American History, Behring Center: Washington, D.C.

Figures 11, 69, and front cover (Father's stone, a/k/a Witchstone) used with permission of the Woodbury Family.

Figure 62 (drawing based on photographs) used with permission of the Nelson-Atkins Museum of Art: Kansas City, Missouri.

ISBN 0-9717910-1-5

First Edition

First Printing - March 2003 - 500 copies

Printed by
Whittier Press, Amesbury MA 01913

To Horace C. Hovey,

Lura W. Watkins,

and Ralph L. Tucker,

whose research made uncovering this story possible.

Table of Contents

PREFACE 1

THE DUMMER FAMILY OF NEWBURY, MASSACHUSETTS 7
    INTRODUCTION 9
    THE FIRST GENERATION 10
    THE SECOND GENERATION 31
    THE THIRD GENERATION 41

THE MERRIMAC VALLEY GRAVESTONE CARVERS 65
    INTRODUCTION 67
    JOHN HARTSHORN (1650 - 1738) 72
    ROBERT MULLICKEN, SR. (1668 - 1741) 82
    ROBERT MULLICKEN, JR. (1688 - 1756) 89
    JOHN MULLICKEN (1690 - 1737) 93
    JOSEPH MULLICKEN (1704 - 1768) 98

THE NEWBURY CARVED STONES 103
    THE CARVED STONES OF THE DUMMER FARM 105
        Introduction 105
        1636 Doorstone 107
        1640 Doorstone 112
        1690 Doorstone 115
        Mother's Stone 121
        Origins of the Designs on the Mother's Stone 128
        Father's Stone 135
    THE MILESTONES IN NEWBURY 142
        Introduction 142
        Milestone 33 145
        Milestone 34 151
        Milestone 35 157
        Milestone 36 161
        Milestone 37 165

CONCLUSION 171

GLOSSARY 177

APPENDIX A - GRAVESTONES USED IN THIS STUDY 178

APPENDIX B - MOTHER'S AND FATHER'S STONE CLUES 182

APPENDIX C - BURYING GROUNDS 183

APPENDIX D 186

Preface

This book is a detailed study of nine stones carved with various decorative art designs. The book focuses on the family who commissioned these carved stones, the artists who carved them, and the decorative artwork that adorns them. All nine carved stones were originally found within the historical boundaries of Newbury, Massachusetts. This collection of nine carved stones is composed of four milestones, four doorstones, and one walkway stone.

Milestones, doorstones, and walkway stones were common in colonial America. They all served a very utilitarian purpose in the everyday lives of the farmers and merchants. Milestones were used along roads to indicate the number of miles to a town. Doorstones served as a step into a house. Walkway stones were stones sunk into the ground along the path leading into the house. They provided solid footing when approaching the house especially when the ground was muddy due to rain or melting snows.

What makes this collection of nine stones stand out amongst all the other stones used for these purposes are their prolific carved decorative art designs. These designs range from highly abstract geometric patterns to human figures. The use of decorative art designs on milestones, doorstones, and walkways during the time period 1636 - 1735 was isolated to the town of Newbury, Massachusetts. All of the surviving examples of milestones, doorstones, and walkway stones from this time period lack artistic embellishment with the exception of these nine stones from Newbury, Massachusetts. This raises a profound question. What unusual historical circumstances in Newbury prompted the creation of these nine uniquely carved stones?

The research on these stones was originally intended to answer a simple question: "Who carved these stones and when?" The research uncovered the answer to this question and much more. The historical circumstances under which these stones came into being were far more complicated and intriguing then it had been imagined. The stones were carved over a ninety year period (1645-1733) and chronicled the lives of three generations of Newbury's leading family: The Dummers. They are the work of seven different stone carvers of whom five are known by name. The events that these stones commemorate span the first century of Newbury's history (1635-1735).

Stories Carved in Stone

The earliest mention of these stones in the historical record comes in John J. Currier's book Ould Newbury published in 1896. Currier included photographs of the milestones and described how in the early 1890's, William Little and N. N. Dummer, members of the local historical society, set upright milestones 36 and 37.

In the fall of 1900, Horace Hovey, a reporter with the *Scientific American Supplement* magazine, hearing about these stones interviewed local residents about them. In addition to the four milestones, Hovey found that Mr. Hale who lived in Byfield, a parish of Newbury, had another four carved stones which were all doorstones. The 1636 and 1640 doorstones were found in the barn foundation on Mr. Hale's farm. In the mud of the cow yard was found a doorstone with a portrait of woman carved on it. The 1690 doorstone was found still functioning in its intended capacity as a step into Mr. Hale's house.

Hovey was the first person to attempt to analyze these stones. He described them in terms of pagan symbolism but offered little in the way of interpreting their meaning. What puzzled him, was how a group of Puritans came to have "pagan" symbols on their stones. He ultimately concluded that the Puritans were simply unaware of their origins. The idea that the designs might be geometric art not pagan symbols never crossed his mind. He also noted that there was a similarity between the designs on the local gravestones carved in the first half of the 1700's and the designs on the milestones and doorstones but did not pursue this line of inquiry any further. This was an important observation; however, it would remain uninvestigated for over ninety years.

In 1962, Mr. and Mrs. Twaddell donated the four doorstones (1636, 1640, 1690, and the woman's portrait) to the Smithsonian Institute. They are currently in the collection of the National Museum of American History.

Lura Watkins, a respected professional historian, was the first person to write a detailed historical study of these stones. Besides the four milestones and four doorstones, Watkins learned of a ninth stone which had a full length portrait of a man dressed in 17th century clothing. This stone had been removed from Mr. Hale's property by the prior owner, Mr. Ambrose, to another property he owned in Newbury. Watkins did not believe that a connection existed between the stones found on Mr. Hale's property and the milestones. For that reason, she focused only on the five stones found on Mr. Hale's property in her two articles on the subject.

Stories Carved in Stone

Watkins noted in her 1963 article that the five carved stones had originated from this one property. She performed an extensive property deed search. This search revealed an important discovery: the property where the stones were found was once the site of the Dummer family mansion house. The Dummer's had been a very prominent family in the 1600 and 1700's in Byfield. This was the first major break through in uncovering the history of these stones.

The research for this book began with a comment by a local historic sign painter who mentioned that he had seen the whorls carved on milestone 37 on some gravestones. A trip to the Sawyer Hill Burying Ground in Newburyport, Massachusetts revealed that the gravestones from the early 1700's and the milestone had more than whorl designs in common. Unaware of Horace Hovey's article, the authors had made the same important discovery.

The meticulously researched studies by Ralph Tucker on the gravestone carvers, John Hartshorn and the Mullicken family, revealed the identity of the men who created the gravestones which had many designs in common with the milestones and the carved stones found on the Dummer property. Tucker's work showed that these carvers changed designs every few years therefore allowing for the dating of specific designs to within a three year time period. Furthermore, each stone carver used different designs.[1] With this information, the remaining undated carved stones could be dated with reasonable accuracy and the carver identified.

By expanding upon Lura Watkin's research on the Dummer family and correlating it to the dates the stones were carved, the purpose and meaning of the various stones were found. Furthermore, the identity of the man and woman whose "portraits" were carved in stone was also revealed.[2]

In piecing together this historical puzzle a fascinating story has emerged. It is first and foremost the history of the Dummer family and their nine carved stones. However, the geometric designs on these nine stones bring to light the artistic traditions which flourished in 17th and early 18th century Puritan New England. And finally, it is about several women who helped to shape the future of their communities and were publicly recognized for their efforts.

---

[1] Gravestone carvers in Merrimac valley region were known to borrow designs ideas from each other. However, it was extremely rare for them to copy the other carver's designs exactly. Instead, the carver would modify the design in some manner.

[2] The word "portraits" is a misnomer because the woman's face is actually a copy of a cherub design from a professionally carved Boston gravestone and the man was copied from a design on an early 1700's ceramic mug.

Author's Note

This research involved an enormous amount of historical information about five stone carvers, three generations of Dummers, the early history of Newbury, and nine carved stones. The task of presenting this information in a readable and organized fashion has been quite a challenge. The story of these stones is presented in three sections: *The Dummer Family of Newbury Massachusetts*, *The Merrimac Valley Gravestone Carvers*, and *The Newbury Carved Stones*. Although each section is a separate subject by itself, they are all inter-twined and related to each other. For the sake of clarity and to avoid repetition of material each section provides a detailed historical analysis of the subject at hand while referring to conclusions discussed in other sections *some of which are later in the book.*

The Dummer Family of Newbury, Massachusetts

Fig. A - The 1636 Doorstone shown in front of an early 1700's New England door.
1636 Doorstone is in the collection of the Smithsonian Institution, National Museum of American History.
Used with permission.

Introduction

The Dummer family played a central role in the creation of a unique and historically important collection of colonial art. This collection of colonial art is composed of nine carved stones: four doorstones, four milestones, and one walkway stone. Two of the stones are the earliest known examples of carved art in colonial America, pre-dating even the first carved gravestones (1647). Carved between 1643 and 1733, these nine stones document the lives of three generations of Dummers, the Parish of Byfield which they helped to found, and the first century of the history of Newbury, Massachusetts.

These nine stones represented more than works of art for the Dummer family, they were a testament to a traditional agricultural way of life which they brought across the Atlantic to the New World. This way of life would be ultimately challenged in the 1700's by the new rising mercantile elite, and the final carved stone would commemorate this struggle. The history of the Dummer family is central to understanding both the purpose of these carved stones and their art.

The First Generation

On April 8, 1632, Richard Dummer and his wife, Mary, embarked on the ship *Whale* and left Hampton, England for the Massachusetts Bay Colony in America. John Winthrop, Governor of the Massachusetts Bay Colony, noted in his journal the arrival of the *Whale* in Boston Harbor on May 26. Dummer's relative, Reverend Stephen Bachiler, aged 71, arrived on June 5 with his family and religious followers aboard the *William and Francis* after having left London on March 9th. The two ships were the second contingent of the ill-fated *Company of Husbandmen* who the previous year had obtained a grant to settle a colony in Maine.[3]

The *Company of Husbandmen* was organized in 1630 as a joint stock company by a small group of London merchants[4] with a capital of £1400. The company obtained a patent (i.e. grant) of land from Sir Ferdinando Gorges to a tract of land along the Sagadahock River in Maine.[5] The first colonists, a meager ten people, arrived in Maine aboard the ship *Plough*. The colonist found the place uninhabitable and removed south to the Massachusetts Bay Colony in the spring of 1631. This failure was further complicated by legal challenges to the company's patent.[6]

Reverend Bachiler arrived in Boston with a letter dated March 8, 1631[/1632] from the Company to the colonists. The letter detailed the legal controversy along with discussing Bachiler's appointment as the religious leader of their society. The letter makes no reference to the failed attempt to colonize the lands in Maine. This is strange in light of the fact that, the captain of the *Plough*, master Graves, returned to Great Britain in time to take command of the *Whale*. Both Dummer and Bachiler were therefore aware of the legal problems and failure of the settlement prior to leaving. This explains why both the *Whale* and the *William and Francis* sailed for Boston rather than Maine.[7]

Both Dummer and Bachiler were investors in the company. Bachiler's motives for joining and investing the company were deeply religious in nature. Dummer's involvement was in part due to family relation. However, his primary motive was a business investment. The

---

[3] Hosmer, 1908: (Vol. 1) 65, 80-81. See also footnotes on pp. 65, 81. The exact relationship between Richard Dummer and Stephen Bachiler [variants: batcheller, Batchelor] is unclear (Weymouth, n.d.).
[4] The merchants included John Dyer, John Roach, Grace Hardwin, and Thomas Jupe.
[5] Present day Portland, Maine.
[6] Hosmer, 1908: (Vol. 1) 65, 80; F. B. Sanborn, 1900; V. C. Sanborn, 1917.

letter states that "Mr. Dummer's promise is also to join with you, *if there be any reason for it.*"[8] Dummer clearly left himself the option of not joining their settlement. With the failure of the *Company of Husbandmen*, Dummer obtained the patent (i.e. land grant) and eventually sold the patent to Mr. Rigby.[9] Within six months after arriving in Boston, Dummer took the Freeman's Oath and became a citizen of the Massachusetts Bay Colony.[10]

Richard Dummer emigrated from Bishopstoke, Great Britain where a branch of the Dummer family had settled. Dummer had come from a country town of farms with a strong agrarian economy where he owned agricultural lands and mill interests.[11] Before leaving he bequeathed a gift to the poor. This is seen in an ancient plaque that hangs in the church in Bishopstoke (Southampton County). It reads in part,

> A memorial of the several Persons who have been Benefactors to the Poor of the Parish of Bishopstoke ... Richard Dummer ... did surrender a CLOSE of LAND called five acres to Stephen Dummer his brother and his heirs with the condition for payment of the like sum of forty Shillings yearly for the Use of the Poor and Needy inhabitants of the said Parish ...[12]

Richard was one of several members of the Dummer family who contributed to the poor. Two other relatives of Richard Dummer did likewise a few years later. The widow Elizabeth Neve (in-law) and Thomas Dummer (Richard's brother) both left money to the poor.[13] Richard Dummer brought to New England both his family's expertise in mills and their sense of generosity.

Shortly after arriving on the *Whale*, Richard and his wife Mary settled in Roxbury, a town near Boston. On November 6, 1632 he took the Freeman's Oath.[14] The next year, in 1633, he built the colony's second water mill in Roxbury.[15] By 1634, Dummer had acquired land not only in Roxbury but also Saugus. On March 4, 1633/4 the General Court reduced the taxes on his

---

[7] Massachusetts Historical Society, 1865: 4th Series, vol. VII, 91-94 (notes).
[8] Massachusetts Historical Society, 1865: 4th Series, vol. VII, 91-94 (notes).
[9] V. C. Sanborn, 1917.
[10] Watkins, 1969: 7. Note: *Freeman* – A male head of household who held full rights of citizenship, including the right to hold office, vote, and engage in business.
[11] Phillips, 1945: 35.
[12] Ewell, 1904: 25-26.
[13] New England Historical and Genealogical Register, October 1892; Ancestors and Descendents of Robert Clements, v 1, 24.
[14] Shurtleff, 1853: (vol.1) 367; Watkins, 1969: 7.

properties in both Roxbury and Saugus.[16] This action may have been prompted by Dummer's large and generous contribution of £30 to the Castle Island Fort. This was £10 more than any other single contributor.[17] On September 3, 1634, he was chosen to oversee the powder and shot and all other ammunition in Roxbury.[18] The following spring, Mr. Dummer and John Johnson were chosen to build a cart bridge over Muddy River in the vicinity of Boston.[19]

Between September 1634 and February 1635, Richard and Mary Dummer traveled to the area that would shortly become the Town of Newbury. (The purpose of this trip will become apparent as the events of the spring of 1635 unfold.) While in Newbury, Mary gave birth to their first son, Shubael, on February 17, 1635. Shortly afterwards, Mary returned to Boston. By May 1635, Richard had returned to Boston at the urgent request of his wife, who was gravely ill. Mary died in the spring of 1635, after being treated unskillfully by Mr. Clark.[20]

According to the Reverend John Elliot, Mary was a follower of Anne Hutchinson. Anne Hutchinson held lectures at her home where she discussed sermons and expressed opinions contrary to established Puritan doctrines. Sometime prior to her death, Mary had persuaded Richard to accept Anne Hutchinson's "opinions."[21] This decision to be associated with Anne Hutchinson would prove to be a near disaster for Richard in subsequent years.

While this was happening, Rev. Thomas Parker had applied to the General Court to start a new plantation (town) north of Ipswich on the Falls River (Parker River), called "Neweberry." On May 6, 1635, the General Court created the plantation of Newbury and gave orders for bounds of the town to be laid out.[22] Three other events occurred at the May 6th session of the General Court that directly affected Dummer. He was chosen as one of the ten Governor's Assistants. Secondly, he was granted up to 500 acres of land at "the falls" in Newbury. This tract of land was located about five miles out from the town center on the south side of the Falls [Parker] River. The land contained fertile soils along the river for agriculture, meadows for

---

[15] Hosmer, 1908: 112. Watkins, 1969: 7.
[16] Shurtleff, 1853: (vol. 1) 112.
[17] Noble, 1904: (Vol. II) 42.
[18] Shurtleff, 1853: (vol. 1) 125; Currier, 1902: 647.
[19] Shurtleff, 1853: (vol. 1) 141.
[20] Currier, 1902: 58-59, 651 note. Much of our information about Richard and Mary Dummer's life from the fall of 1634 to the spring of 1635 comes from the Reverend John Elliot's records of the church members in Roxbury. Currier quotes the relevant passages in a footnote.
[21] Currier, 1902: 651 note.
[22] Currier, 1902: 30.

sheep, cattle, and horses, forest for wood and the nearby water falls offered a place for a mill. Thirdly, the residents living in the towns of Watertown and Roxbury were given liberty to move where ever they pleased.[23]

Two Dutch ships from Holland, arrived in Boston on June 3, 1635 with 27 horses, 63 heifers, and 88 sheep.[24] This livestock was the property of a joint stock company involved in a livestock venture. Richard Dummer, Henry Saltonstall, and Henry Sewall were amongst the investors.[25] Mr. Dummer and Mr. Bartholemewe were chosen by the General Court to set apart, "a convenient quantity of land" for the livestock on July 8, 1635.[26] The land for the cattle was laid out near "The Falls" where both Dummer and Sewall had their grants of land.[27] Saltonstall contracted with Thomas Coleman to care for the cattle at Newbury. By November 3, 1635 it became apparent that Coleman had not done his job. The General Court noted that many of the livestock had died due to his negligence. The General Court allowed the investors to seize some of the company's assets, in particular the oats and hay so that they may, "take care of their cattell for the winter."[28]

The same day (July 8, 1635) that Richard Dummer was granted rights to lay out land for the cattle, Dummer and John Spencer were granted the right to build a mill and fish weir at "The Falls." As part of an agreement with the Town of Newbury, both Dummer and Spencer were to receive 60 acres of land each along with timber rights in exchange for building the mill. This was most likely a saw mill.[29] It was common practice for the newly established towns to provide incentives for the building of grist and sawmills.

Mr. Dummer had the legal right to move out to Newbury in 1635 but did not. He stayed in Roxbury until February 1636. Dummer remained active in government affairs in Boston for the remainder of 1635. He attended the court sessions as one of the Governor's Assistants

---

[23] Shurtleff, 1853: (vol. 1) 145-146.
[24] Hosmer, 1908:152.
[25] Watkins, 1969: 8; Currier, 1902: 32-33.
[26] Shurtleff, 1853: (vol. 1) 149.
[27] Coffin, 1845: 18.
[28] Currier, 1902: 33. Shurtleff, 1853: (vol. 1) 155.
[29] Watkins, 1969: 8-9; Currier, 1902: 648.

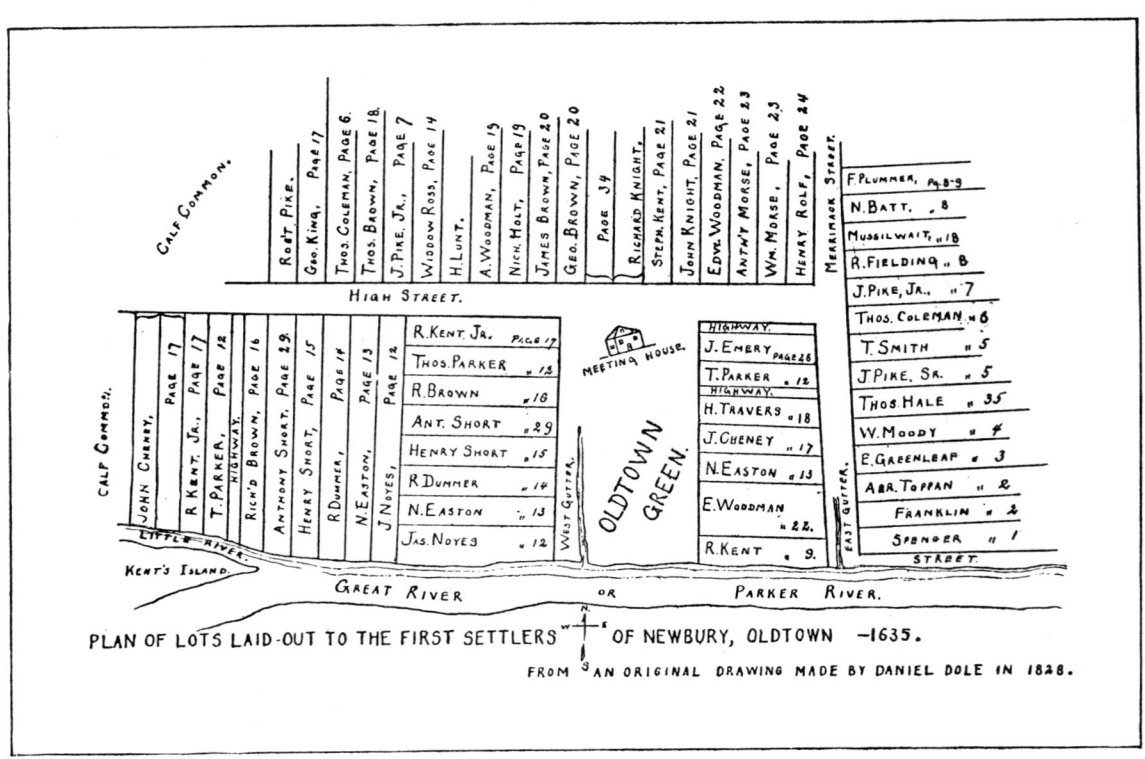

Fig. 1 – Map of Newbury's 1635 town layout.
Reprinted from J. J. Currier's, *Ould Newbury*, Boston, MA: Damrell & Upham, 1896.

(June 2, July 7, August 4, September 1, and November 3). In September he was authorized to buy the lead for Castle Island Fort and to swear in a constable for the Town of Newbury.[30]

The year 1636 proved to be a busy year for Dummer. Dummer seems to have split his time between Newbury where he attended to both his personal and government affairs, and Boston where he attended the General Court and Quarterly Court sessions (March 1 & 3, April 5, May 25, June 7, September 7 & 8, December 6 & 7).[31] Dummer made upwards of six trips between Newbury and Boston as evidenced by the various court sessions he attended in Boston.

In February 1636, Newbury town records show he first leased a two acre house lot on the lower green and another two acre river front lot for his cattle (See fig. 1). He was forced to lease the lots because of a law enacted in September 1635 prohibited settlers from building a house beyond a half-mile of the meeting house.[32] His farm was about five miles distance from the meeting house. By September 1636, he had completed the building of a mill at "The Falls."[33] John Spencer, who shared the original mill rights with Dummer, was never mentioned after the initial grant. It is unknown what transpired in this business partnership or how Dummer came to own it outright.[34]

Shortly after he moved out to Newbury, a plantation [town] was ordered to be set out at Hampton [NH]. On the same day (March 3, 1636), he and Mr. Spencer were given the power to choose a convenient location and hire men to build the meeting house in Hampton.[35] Both Dummer and Spencer were expected to bear the initial expenses for the meeting house construction. Afterwards they were to be reimbursed, "& what money they lay out aboute it shalbe repaide them out of the treasury, or by that who come to inhabite there."[36] The colony chose wealthy individuals like Dummer for these projects primarily because of their ability to finance the project out of their own pockets. On May 25, 1636, Mr. Dummer and three other men were appointed magistrates [judges] for the Ipswich and Newbury courts. Mr. Dummer was also

---

[30] Shurtleff, 1853: (vol. 1) 150-152, 154-155, 158.
[31] Shurtleff, 1853: (vol. 1) 163, 164, 167, 171, 173, 176, 177, 184.
[32] Currier, 1896: 14, 313; Currier, 1902: 39.
[33] Watkins, 1969: 8-9.
[34] Currier, 1902: 38-39.
[35] Shurtleff, 1853: (vol. 1) 167.
[36] Ibid.

chosen as the colony's treasurer at the same time.[37] He would serve as the treasurer for a one year term (May 1636 to May 1637).

To encourage the new settlers to build a house on their in-town lots, the land was leased or granted with the condition it be built on within six months.[38] It appears Richard built a house, because in November 1637 he was notified his lease had expired and the town compensated him as required by the terms of the lease agreement.[39] The town's decision not to renew Dummer's lease coincided with him being condemned for holding the same religious opinions as Mrs. Anne Hutchinson. She and sixty of her followers fell into disfavor with the colony and were ordered to turn in their guns and ammunition. However, the General Court stated that any person who admitted to their "sin" would not be disarmed.[40] Dummer surrendered his weapons and sailed back to England.[41]

Richard Dummer's decision to accept disarmament rather than renounce his religious views was a risky decision. Granted, he seemed to realize the disarmament decision was a temporary punishment and that the government officials needed a cooling off period. However, he jeopardized his personal reputation as a gentleman, the success of his business ventures, and his political appointments within the government.

Little is known of Richard Dummer's religious views. The extent of his association with Stephen Bachiler's small religious sect is not completely clear. Initially he separated himself from Bachiler upon arrival in Boston. Dummer first settled in Roxbury and Bachiler moved to Saugus. Due to a religious disagreement, Bachiler moved from Saugus to Newbury where his son-in-law, Christopher Hussey, and his relative, Richard Dummer, had moved to. Bachiler's residence in Newbury was temporary. He petitioned for and was granted the right to settle the town of Hampton [NH].[42] Richard Dummer was one of the two gentlemen chosen to lay out the bounds of Hampton and to build its meeting house. Dummer's involvement with Bachiler most likely stemmed from a sense of family obligation only. Interestingly enough, Stephen Bachiler never associated himself with Anne Hutchinson.

---

[37] Shurtleff, 1853: (vol. 1) 175.
[38] Watkins, 1969: 12.
[39] Currier, 1896: 315.
[40] Shurtleff, 1853: (vol. 1) 211-212.
[41] Currier, 1902: 38, 648-649.
[42] V. C. Sanborn, 1917.

Richard Dummer's association with Anne Hutchinson is well documented. He apparently agreed to some extent with Hutchinson's religious opinions because he chose not to renounce them. The Hutchinson affair illustrates another important aspect of Richard's character. Dummer was one of a number of men who were associated with Anne Hutchinson. By refusing to renounce Anne Hutchinson and her opinions, Dummer was publicly declaring his support and his respect for her. The idea of men publicly acknowledging and supporting a woman was contrary to the prevailing attitude of the 1600's which treated woman as second class citizens. This attitude, largely derived from the Bible's command that women be obedient to their husbands, may have been an ideal of the Puritan religion rather than a reality. As the story of the Dummer family unfolds, a pattern of men publicly acknowledging their respect and support for woman emerges.

Dummer took advantage of the turmoil over the Hutchinson affair, and sailed to England. In May of 1638, Richard returned to the colony aboard the *Bevis*. On this trip, he was accompanied by his brother, Stephen, his brother's wife, Alice, their three children, three other members of the Dummer family and ten servants, which included a carpenter, tailor and baker.[43] On August 6th, the selectmen of Newbury made an agreement with Richard Dummer, to encourage him to fit his mill to grind corn. In exchange for adding a grist mill to his existing sawmill, the Town agreed not to grant any other grist mills in town. Dummer completed fitting his mill to grind corn sometime between 1638 and 1645. Newbury town records indicated that there was a grist mill at "The Falls" in 1645.[44] On September 21, 1638 the town offered him a second house lot, "There is granted to mr Richard Dummer halfe an acre [of] ground for an houselott next to Henry Travers on condition that he build on it within halfe an yeere." And according to historian Lura Watkins, "He apparently did not do so for, on October 6, he acquired a house from Thomas Hale, with land on both sides of Merrimack ridge."[45]

Dummer's involvement in the Hutchinson affair cost him political appoints for several years. From November 1637 to April 1640 Mr. Dummer's name does not appear in the General Court Records. This all changes at the May 13, 1640 General Court meeting, when elections for

---

[43] Tepper, 1978: 49-50.
[44] Currier, 1902: 38-39, 156, 649; Watkins, 1969: 9.
[45] Watkins, 1969: 12.

Stories Carved in Stone

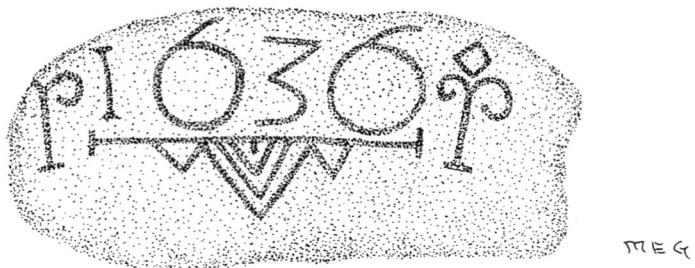

Fig. 2 – 1636 Doorstone carved for Richard Dummer Sr. acknowledging the year he settled in the Town of Newbury.
1636 Doorstone is in the collection of the Smithsonian Institution, National Museum of American History. Used with permission.

Fig. 3 - 1640 Doorstone carved for Richard Dummer Sr. with the date he built a house on his farm near "The Falls" in Newbury.
1640 Doorstone is in the collection of the Smithsonian Institution, National Museum of American History. Used with permission.

the coming year were held. Mr. Dummer was reinstated by being appointed to assist the magistrates at Ipswich.[46] Winthrop's severe financial loss of £2500 was also discussed at the May 13, 1640 meeting. The General Court opted to solicit voluntary contributions to help Winthrop. A total of £500 was raised of which £100 was donated by Richard Dummer. The remainder of the funds were donated by Boston and several other towns.[47] Dummer's return to government appointed positions was probably directly influenced by his generous contribution.

On the same day, the court repealed the law that prohibited building a house beyond a half-mile of the meeting house.[48] This made it possible for Richard to build a house on his farm property out near the falls where his mill was located. No historical reference to when he built his house at the farm has been found. However, a doorstone found on his farm with the date 1640 and fleur-de-lis is a strong indication he built that year. (See Fig. 3)

The doorstone was carved between 1640 and 1645. It pre-dates the earliest gravestone carved in New England which is dated 1647.[49] The date 1640 must have been significant to Richard Dummer. He chose 1640 rather *than* 1635 which is the date he acquired the property at "The Falls." The manor house Mr. Dummer built at the farm proved to be his permanent residence. It seems reasonable to argue that 1640 represents the year he built his residence on the property.

Dummer was in charge of the weights and measures for the Town of Newbury. At the June 2, 1640 meeting of the General Court Dummer was fined for lack of weights and scales. The fine was later rescinded when it was realized that the original charge was incorrect.[50] In September 1640, Richard bought another five hundred acre farm in Watertown.[51] Nothing is mentioned again about it beyond the fact he still owned it as of 1659, according to a court hearing in Watertown.[52] On October 7, he was appointed to the position of Deputy (for Essex County) in the General Court. On the same day he was also appointed as a magistrate for Newbury.[53]

---

[46] Currier, 1902: 39.
[47] Hosmer, 1908: (vol. 2) 3-4.
[48] Currier, 1902: 39.
[49] Ipswich Cemetery, gravestone reads "EL 1647".
[50] Shurtleff, 1853: (vol. 1) 297, 315.
[51] Currier, 1902: 649; Suffolk Deeds 1885: (vol. 1), 13.
[52] Currier, 1902: 649.
[53] Shurtleff, 1853: (vol. 1) 301, 307-308.

On June 2, 1641, Dummer was appointed to assist the Ipswich court and on December 10, 1641 he was appointed as a magistrate for Newbury.[54] During this year, Richard (who was still a widower) arranged the marriage of his brother, Thomas's daughter, Joan Dummer Sprinter to Thomas Nelson of Rowley [MA]. He paid Joan's dowry of two hundred pounds. However, before giving it to Mr. Nelson he wrote a marriage contract whereby Joan would receive double that amount (i.e. 400 pounds) if her husband died first and left her a widow.[55] This would potentially provide Joan with more income than she would have derived from receiving 1/3 of her husband's estate as proscribed by the law. In this time period, with its uncertainty of life expectancy, Richard had the forethought to make provisions for his niece should she become a widow.

Richard not only assisted his family but was called upon by friends, too. Robert Muzzey of Ipswich, names four men in his will to oversee his estate. Two of the four men were chosen to finish raising his children. On January 5, 1642, Mr. Dummer was given the responsibility of Joseph Muzzey. Mr. Norton was given Benjamin and Mary. Their education was of primary importance to Robert Muzzey. He felt his wife could not give them a proper education. He referred to Mr. Dummer and Mr. Norton as friends.[56] The Muzzey case is one of three in which Mr. Dummer was asked to take over the "education" of other peoples children upon death. John Spencer (6/1/1637) and Thomas Nelson (12/24/1645) were the other two people who chose him.[57] When Mr. Dummer was called upon to defend his authority as executor of Thomas Nelson's estate, he gave a full and complete account of the expenses he incurred to the Salem Court. These expenses included mill renovations, setting up a farm to be rented out, and the education and care of Phillip & Thomas Nelson. Dummer listed the names of several teachers and mentions others that were hired to teach the boys. In another account that Dummer gave to the probate court (1656), he mentions that one of the Nelson boys was sent off to college and the other was working for him for wages.[58]

In 1643, Richard married Frances Burr, the widow of Rev. Jonathan Burr of Boston. Frances, who already had four children, brought them with her to the farm in Newbury. She was

---

[54] Shurtleff, 1853: (vol. 1) 328, 345
[55] Essex County MA, 1916: (vol. 1) 113; Essex County MA, 1912: (vol. 2) 8-20.
[56] Essex County MA, 1916: (vol. 1) 30.
[57] Essex County MA, 1916: (vol. 1) 107, 110.
[58] Essex County, MA, 1912: (vol. 2) 15; Essex County, MA: 1916: (vol. 1) 115-116.

in her early thirties, still young enough to have more children. Two years later, she gave birth to a son, Jeremiah, on July 14, 1645.[59]

Over in Rowley in January 1644, Thomas Nelson was granted land at Mill Field in exchange for building a mill. In Nelson's will, dated December 24, 1645, he leaves to his wife, Joan, "….my Mill, mill houses, with the appurtenances."[60] Nelson built a gristmill before his death. The mill was about a mile from Dummer's farm. Richard Holmes, a mill-wright, was hired to build the gristmill. Holmes states, "... I wrought at above said Mills, at Mr Nellsons Charge, to build said Mills & Dams & make ye stones for said Grist Mill...."[61] Mark Prime was hired to operate the mill.[62] There is no record of who Dummer hired to build and operate his own grist mill at "The Falls." However, it is possible it was the same two workmen that Nelson had employed.

Between 1640-1645, Dummer had the first of two doorstones carved for his manor house on the farm. The historical record indicates that there were at least two workmen capable doing the carving on this first doorstone: Richard Holmes and Mark Prime. Holmes made the stones for Nelson's grist mill. Prime who was hired to operate the Nelson mill, needed the skills to sharpen the mill stones. During peak operation, the mill stones would need to be sharpened approximately every two weeks.[63] As previously mentioned, the first doorstone was carved with the date 1640. It had two upside down fleur-de-lis carved on it in addition to the date. The upside down designs may have been a mistake. However, the most likely explanation is that they were a political statement of some sort.

Between the years 1650 and 1652, Mr. Dummer (as executor of Nelson's estate) made improvements to Nelson's mill. This included installing two new grindstones imported from England. Once he had the stones at the mill, he hired a Mr. Funnell to cut and shape the millstones. It would appear they were shipped over in a roughed out shape and finished at the mill site. Mark Prime and a Mr. Law were also paid for working on the millstones (probably for

---

[59] Watkins, 1969: 12.
[60] Gage, 1840: 410.
[61] Jewett and Jewett, 1946: 170-171.
[62] Essex County MA, 1912: (vol. 2) 20-21.
[63] Watkins, 1963: 423. Watkins, 1969: 13. Watkins was the first historian to suggest that 1636 & 1640 doorstones were carved by millwrights or mill workers.

sharpening them). Dummer also paid Prime for four months work on maintaining the mill dam. After the renovation work, Dummer rented the mill to an unspecified person.[64]

Between 1645 and 1679, Richard had a second doorstone carved with the date 1636. (See fig. 2) On this doorstone the fleur-de-lis are in the upright position and a design of triangles was carved underneath the date. It commemorates the year he first settled in the town of Newbury. Like the 1640 doorstone, the 1636 doorstone was most likely carved by a millwright. However, the evidence suggests that the two were done by different millwrights. The carver had good artistic ability, but, he tilted the fleur-de-lis at a slight outward angle whereas the fleur-de-lis on the 1640 doorstone are straight up and down.

The two doorstones were more than just commemorative stones marking the dates that he first settled at Newbury and built his manor house at the farm. The doorstones were part of a larger social trend amongst the upper class society of England. The region from which Dummer immigrated from in England had a number of country estate buildings with dates, heraldic devices (coat-of-arms), and decorative geometric art designs incorporated into the exterior walls. These decorative embellishments to the buildings were intended for public display. In addition, many of the churches had commemorative and memorial plaques hanging on their walls. The doorstones embodied all of these concepts.

Fig. 4 – Dummer Family Coat-of-Arms.

---

[64] Essex County MA. 1912: (vol. 2) 19.

The fleur-de-lis symbol comes from the Dummer coat-of-arms. (See fig. 4) Armorial or heraldic devices (coat of arms) were another means to display an upper class person's heritage and were commonly incorporated into the stonework, chimneys, fireplaces and porch entrances on houses and public buildings. By the late sixteenth and early seventeenth centuries, during Richard Dummer, Sr.'s life in England, this use of heraldry on privately owned buildings reached its height.[65] Dummer, when he had his doorstones carved with the fleur-de-lis, did what was familiar to him. He displayed a symbol from his own coat-of-arms on his house.

Both the 1636 and 1640 doorstone commemorated important events in the Dummer family. This also has its counter part in England. In the town of Dummer, England in the early 1500's a wealthy Dummer ancestor of Richard's had a beautiful brass plaque hung in the town's church.[66] According to researcher, D. G. Weymouth many of members of the Dummer family resided in, "South Stoneham or Swathling, where the ancient church bears several Dummer memorials."[67] Prior to sailing to New England, Richard Dummer had arranged for the support of the poor in Bishopstoke. A plaque was hung in the church denoting that contribution.

The 1636 doorstone has a geometric triangular design on it. This type of design is referred to as decorative art. Decorative art designs pervaded many aspects of life during the 1600's. Various designs could be found on furniture, ceramic dishware, and the more expensive items made from pewter and silver. The particular triangular design found on the 1636 can be traced back to similar triangular patterns incorporated into the roofing (tile, slate, or thatch) of some English houses.[68]

Although these designs and embellishments were popular in England, they were largely frowned upon by the conservative Puritan values. The household items that have survived from the 1600's indicate that items with decorative artwork were acceptable within the private realm of family household.[69] Architectural studies of New England buildings up to 1675-80 indicate the exteriors of the buildings were plain and unornamented.[70] The exterior of buildings were within the public realm and so were the doorstones. Richard Dummer's doorstones reflect

---

[65] Friar, 1987: 128-129.
[66] Ewell, 1904: 31.
[67] Weymouth, n.d.
[68] See the section the 1636 doorstone for more details and citations.
[69] *For examples see* Stillinger, 1972: 3-62.
[70] Cummings, 1979:126-127.

common trends of the upper class, especially in England, yet at the same time they reflect a certain amount of defiance of Puritan values.

Prior to his involvement with Nelson's estate, Dummer was active in government affairs. From 1640 to 1649, Dummer was busy with his duties as deputy, magistrate and the person chosen to end small controversies. (See appendix for years) During that time he was appointed to several committees. Most of the committees dealt with ordinary business like laying out towns, and writing ordinances for trading posts. Two of the committees involved internal matters dealing with the General Court. Dummer and two others were chosen to write up an order to prevent house members from disclosing private court business outside with the general public. They were also given the duty to write a second ordinance, to prevent anyone from passing false rumors. On another occasion he was part of a committee appointed to write a third ordinance for in-house use at the General Court. "…to consider of some way whereby ye negative vote may be tempered, yt justice may have free passage, …"[71]

At the May 2, 1649 General Court Session, Dummer petitioned the court to relieve him of his duties in order to act as executor of Nelson's estate.[72] This date marks the end of his participation in the General Court. It does not end his public duties. In September 1653 his name appears again. He was appointed to the County Court at Hampton [NH] as a magistrate.[73] The settlement of Nelson's estate took several more years and included two court suits before it was settled.[74]

Richard and Frances continued to add to their family. They had a son Jeremiah born on July 14, 1645, a daughter Hannah born November 7, 1647, Richard Jr. born on January 13, 1649, and Nathaniel whose birth date is unknown.[75] Nathaniel sadly drowned in a boating accident in 1658.[76] They had one more child, a son, William born January 18, 1659.[77]

There are no early records discussing the education of Dummer's sons. The teachers Dummer hired to educate the Nelson boys undoubtedly also taught Dummer's children. When Richard, Sr.'s first son, Shubael came of age for formal education, he sent him to Harvard

---

[71] Shurtleff, 1853: (vol. 3) 7, 11.
[72] Shurtleff, 1853: (vol. 2) 272.
[73] Shurtleff, 1853: (vol. 4 pt. 1) 180.
[74] Essex county MA, 1916: (vol. 1) 114-116.
[75] Watkins, 1969: 12.
[76] Essex County MA, 1912: (vol. 2) 119.

University.[78] In 1656, Shubael graduated and became a minister in York, Maine.[79] In 1659, when Jeremiah was about fourteen years old, he apprenticed him to John Hull, the noted silversmith in Boston.[80] Jeremiah remained in Boston for the rest of his life after becoming the first America born silversmith and later, the father of Lt. Governor William Dummer.[81]

Up until the early 1650's, the only way to travel from Rowley to Newbury was to take a long circuitous route out around the falls. About 1654, this changed when Richard Thurlow built a bridge over the Falls (Parker) River. This was located about a mile or so down from the actual falls and shortened the route by going through the lower part of Dummer's farm from Rowley to Newbury. The shorter route via Thurlow's bridge became apart of the colony's Bay Road (Middle Road).[82] Used by government officials, post riders, soldiers, farmers, craftsmen and travelers alike the Bay Road formed an important link in the colony. As a single continuous route, it connected Boston to all the northern towns up to Newbury. Beyond Newbury it connected to the King's Highway which ended in Portsmouth, New Hampshire.

Richard on at least one occasion loaned money for property mortgages. William Phillips obtained a loan for 78 pounds and 15 shillings from Dummer for a one acre lot on the outskirts of Boston. The mortgage is dated October 28, 1659. Phillips had until March 26, 1660 to pay off the loan.[83] No record of the final outcome of this arrangement has been found.

By 1660, Richard's cattle herd had grown so large and aggressive they became a problem in Rowley. This prompted Rowley's people to take the matter into their own hands and vote to put up, "A substantial and strong three-railed fence...between Newbury and Rowley, to prevent cattle coming from Mr. Dummer's farm."[84]

In January 1668, Richard Dummer and John Pearson petitioned the Quarterly Court at Salem for reimbursement of expenses incurred in rebuilding the bridge at "The Falls." The expenses included hiring two workman and supplies. Apparently this is not the first time the

---

[77] Watkins, 1969: 12.
[78] Watkins, 1969: 10.
[79] Currier, 1902: 518.
[80] Watkins, 1969: 12.
[81] Phillips, 1945: 38-39. NOTE: Several examples of Jeremiah's silver pieces are in the collection of the Museum of Fine Arts in Boston.
[82] Jewett and Jewett, 1946: 158-159.
[83] Suffolk County MA, 1885: (vol. 3) 513.
[84] Ewell, 1904: 48.

bridge had to be rebuilt. The account makes reference two other men having rebuilt the bridge the previous year.[85]

For more than twenty years there was an ongoing dispute about how Rev. Parker ran the Newbury Church. The dispute was not about his doctrine and preaching, it was over his view of church government. It is best summed up by testimony given by Richard Bartlett, James Ordway and John Emery on March 30, 1669. "We testify that Mr. Parker in a public meeting said that for the time to come I am resolved nothing shall be brought into the church, but it shall be brought first to me, and if I approve of it, it shall be brought in, if I do not approve it, it shall not be brought in." Edward Woodman was the leader of the group opposing Rev. Parker. Several of Rev. Parker's supporters testified that Woodman had denounced Parker by saying the reverend had "more power than the pope." What these men were saying was Rev. Parker had set himself up as a dictator of the Newbury Church. This divided the church in half, half favoring Rev. Parker and the other half being against him.[86]

Richard Dummer was one of those who opposed Rev. Parker's dictates. In 1671, Richard's involvement in the Rev. Parker dispute escalated. He was appointed president of Woodman's Group. Mr. Dummer and Mr. Thurlow as elders were called upon to write up a formal complaint.[87] Woodman's Group at this time made an attempt to oust Rev. Parker. The court eventually sided in favor of Rev. Parker as the church official. Woodman's Group was given small fines. The court decision officially ended the dispute but discontentment continued for many years afterward.

Dummer continued to expand his land holdings throughout the 1650's and 1660's. In May 1656, Dummer petitioned the General Court for an 800 acre grant in exchange for £73 worth of contributions made to the colony in 1637 and 1639. The petition was granted.[88] However, it appears the land was not laid out and given to him until circa 1663. At the General Court session in June that year a record of a land grant of 800 acres is entered. The land is located on the Merrimac River in Billerica.[89] He also bought for £10 a small seven acre plot

---

[85] Essex County MA, 1912: (vol. 3) 99.
[86] Coffin, 1845: 73-74.
[87] Essex County MA, 1912: (vol. 4) 350-366.
[88] Shurtleff, 1853: (vol. 3) 413, (vol. 4, pt. 1) 272.
[89] Shurtleff, 1853: (vol. 4, pt. 2) 79.

from Old Will an Indian from Newbury on March 31, 1663.[90] In another petition dated May 23, 1666 he asked the General Court to grant him a 500 acre farm. This request was granted.[91] Dummer also established three tenant farms on his Newbury farm which he leased out. The first mention of the tenant farms is in a 1673 court proceeding.[92] In the court records dated September 28, 1675, the names of the three tenant farmers are given: Benjamin Goodrich, Duncan Stewart, and R. Robinson.[93] According to testimony given by Robinson, the terms of the lease required the tenant to clear, cultivate, and fence the land and deliver 1/3 of the harvest to the Dummer family. Both Benjamin Goodrich and Duncan Stewart were still tenant farmers in 1680. They were both mentioned in a deed dated November 23, 1680.[94]

Richard Dummer got into a protracted legal suit with the Town of Newbury over the bounds and location of his various properties during the 1670's. The dispute was over the bounds of Dummer's original land grants from the 1630's & 1640's along with Dummer's claims to a tract of land on Plum Island. The matter was settled by arbitration. The Town yielded to most of Dummer's claims for his farm boundaries in exchange for him dropping his claims to land on Plum Island.[95]

Acreage	Location	Town	Reference
300	Farm at Falls	Newbury	Essex County MA, 1912: (vol. 1) 40-41.
170	Farm at Falls	Newbury	Ibid.
50	Saw Mill	Newbury	Ibid, Watkins, 1969: 11.
10	Meadows near farm	Newbury	Watkins, 1969: 11.
300	Main village	Newbury	Ibid.
7	Near the farm	Newbury	Coffin, 1845: 362.
500	T. Mayhew farm	Watertown	Currier, 1902: 649.
800	Merrimac River	Billerica	Shurtleff, 1853: (vol. 4, pt. 2) 79.
500	[Land Grant]	unknown	Shurtleff, 1853: (vol. 4, pt. 2) 306.
???		Saugus	Shurtleff, 1853: (vol. 1) 112.
???		Roxbury	Ibid.
2637 +	Total Acreage		

Fig. 5 – Documented land holdings of Richard Dummer, Sr.

---

[90] Coffin, 1845: 362.
[91] Shurtleff, 1853: (vol. 4, pt. 2) 306. The wording of the record is difficult to understand until the modern equivalent of the old English is inserted "…the court judgeth it meete [fitting, proper] to grant to the peticoner & his heirs heires five hundred acres of land …"
[92] Essex County MA, 1912: (vol. 1) 40.
[93] Essex County MA, 1912: (vol. 5) 64-66.
[94] Watkins, 1969: 17.
[95] Essex County MA, 1912: (vol. 1) 40-41.

Richard, in his later years, was appointed two years in a row (March 6, 1671 and March 4, 1672) "to attend to the prudential affairs of the town."[96]

In the year 1673, Richard, then in his seventy's, divided his estate up and deeded it to his sons as a gift. The first gift went to Richard, Jr., "for his incoragement & advancement & for the makeing good & fullfilling a p'mise & convenant made to & with Capt. John Appleton of Ipswich upon the consideration of a Mariage to be had & compleated between my sd son, Richard Dumer and Mrs. Elizabeth Appleton the eldest daughter of th sd Capt. John Appleton ..."[97] The two fathers, who prearranged this marriage, were able to bring together two young people from two wealthy upper class families. This not only encouraged a marriage, it also was a way of ensuring Richard, Jr. would remain on the farm and have a family to carry on the Dummer legacy. The gift consisted of the mansion house and the land it was on, a total of one hundred and fifty acres. It also included another one hundred fifty acres of unenclosed [not fenced] ground nearby. Richard, Jr. married Elizabeth on November 2, 1673 and inherited his father's house and lands.[98]

The rest of the estate was divided amongst Shubael and William. Dummer's other son, Jeremiah who did not receive a gift of land, purchased part of his father's land. However, when William died before coming of age, Jeremiah received his portion of the estate.[99] Shubael, died February 5, 1691 in York, Maine when he was shot by an Indian during a raid on the town. His portion of land reverted back to the other brothers.[100]

Richard, aware his health was failing, wrote his will on April 23, 1679. He gave his wife Frances the use of one-half of the house, his part of the income from the saw mill, all the household items remaining in his possession, the small stock of cattle and sheep he had retained, and all his riding horses.[101] By previous arrangement Frances also received the income and harvest from William's land until he came of age and 1/3 of it there after. A similar provision was attached to Shubael's earlier gift of land.[102] Richard appointed Elizabeth Paine (his daughter-in-law) guardian of his wife Frances and her inheritance. It is clear that Richard made detailed

---

[96] Currier 1902, 110.
[97] Watkins, 1969: 15.
[98] Watkins, 1969: 15, 20.
[99] Watkins, 1969: 16, 17.
[100] Currier, 1902: 518.
[101] Essex County MA, 1912: (vol. 11) 514-515.

plans for the support and comfort of his wife after his death. Elizabeth Paine was also given full authority to manage and dispose of Frances's inheritance at her own discretion.[103] Richard clearly placed a large amount of trust and responsibility with Elizabeth.

Richard, Sr. died December 14, 1679 and is buried in First Parish Burying Ground. His short, thick, reddish colored gravestone is still there. The years have taken their toll and part of the lettering has flaked off. His gravestone was shaped and lettered by a skilled person but lacks artwork. (See Fig. 6) Richard Dummer, Sr.'s intelligence and integrity helped shape the colony. He lived a long life, "... and he died in a good old age, full of days, riches and honor."[104]

Fig. 6 – Richard Dummer Sr.'s 1679 gravestone in First Parish Burying Ground, Newbury, MA. His headstone was carved by a professional but lacks artwork.

---

[102] Watkins, 1969: 16.
[103] Essex County MA, 1912: (vol. 11) 514-515.
[104] Ewell, 1904: 51.

Richard, Sr.'s wife, Frances remained on the farm and lived in the mansion house until her death on November 19, 1682. The inventory taken of her possessions lists only her personal belongings.[105] The livestock and household items left to her by Richard are noticeably absent from the inventory. It is likely she gave her other possessions to Elizabeth and Richard, Jr. who cared for her after the death of her husband. Frances's inventory "shows that she was plentifully supplied with clothing and personal belongings suited to her position as a 'lady' and not a mere farmer's wife."[106] Frances was buried in First Parish in front of her husband and was given a stone marker. Her short, thick, plain gravestone was made by a different craftsman than her husband's. This is evidenced by the letter "u" which is shaped with slanted sides approximating a "V." Her stone reads:

Mrs FRANCIS DVMER DIED
IN THE 70 YEAR OF HER
AGE -----19 DAY OF
NOVEMBER 1682

---

[105] Essex County MA, 1912 (vol. 11) 514-515. See Watkins, 1969: 18-19 for easily readable copy of the inventory.
[106] Watkins, 1969: 18.

The Second Generation

Richard Dummer, Jr. upon his marriage to Elizabeth in 1673 had inherited his father's farm and mansion house. The mansion was split into two living quarters as evidenced by Richard Dummer Sr.'s will that gave ½ the house to his wife.[107] When Richard, Jr.'s mother, Frances, died he had been married almost ten years. He and his wife, Elizabeth by that date had had several children; Hannah born August 12, 1674, John, born August 8, 1676, Richard, born June 22, 1680 and Elizabeth, born July 20, 1682.[108]

Richard, Jr.'s public activities begin in the spring of 1675 at age 25 when he was appointed as a juror, called "Jury of Trials" at the county court of Ipswich (March 30, 1675, March 29, 1681, Sept. 30, 1684).[109] At age 28, he took the freeman's oath (March 26, 1678.)[110] The next year his name appears in the town records when he was chosen a tithing man (March 31, 1679, April 25, 1681, 1682, 1684).[111] He was chosen for selectman (March 1, 1680, March 13, 1683). He was "appointed [one of the] standing way wardens to see that every inhabitant do their part on the hye wayes [highways]" (March 7, 1681, March 13, 1683).[112] These were common public positions held by many men in the community. With the exception of the county position of juror all others were town positions.

As one of the selectman in 1680 he was involved with a petition to the General Court in regards to the town's schoolmaster's salary. On April 13, 1680 they voted to give twenty pounds to pay for a schoolmaster. Apparently the selectmen found this was inadequate because four months later they petitioned the General Court to be able to raise the amount. On July 11, 1680 the General Court in answer to a petition by the town of Newbury, gave the selectmen the right to raise sixty pounds for the schoolmaster's salary through the town's inhabitants.[113]

---

[107] Essex County MA, 1912: (vol. 11) 514-515.
[108] Watkins, 1969: 20.
[109] Essex County MA, 1912: (vol. 6) 403, (vol. 8) 65, (vol. 9) 311.
[110] Shurtleff, 1853: (vol. 6) 403.
[111] Currier, 1902: 111. Note: "tithing man" – A person appointed by the local selectman to enforce the mandatory attendance of religious service on the Sabbath (pp. 116-117).
[112] Currier, 1902: 111-112.
[113] Currier, 1896: 105; Shurtleff, 1853: (vol. 5) 272.

As part of another committee he was appointed to solve a dispute with Mr. Thurlow over the Newbury [Thurlow] bridge. It seems Mr. Thurlow repaired the bridge but had trouble being paid by the town for his work. In turn, he put up a "stop" by the gate.[114]

Richard Dummer, Jr. like his father publicly supported a woman in her particular endeavor. In May of 1680, he was one four selectman who issued two petitions to the Salem Court on behalf of Mrs. Anne White. Anne White was seeking a license to continue operating her husband's tavern after his death. Richard and the other selectmen went to some lengths to secure the license for Mrs. White. (SEE: "Anne White Petition" for more details.)

[*Second Generation* Chapter continues on page 37]

---

[114] Essex County MA, 1912: (vol. 7) 363.

The Anne White Petition

On May 13, 1680 Mrs. White paid 40 shillings to be able to sell wine and liquor. On May 27, 1680 the selectmen of Newbury petitioned the court on her behalf. According to the court records, the selectmen felt "that Mrs. Anne White should be continued to sell wine and liquor according to the license formerly granted to Capt. Paul White and `because she finds some disturbance we desire that if there may be any way found to secure her selling a afforsayd till the next County court at Salem, when her licence may be farther enlarged, it may be effectually done.'"[115] On May 29, 1680 the selectmen submitted a second petition. Apparently, the court requested that the selectmen justify their request. In the second petition the selectmen argued their case, "considering that the town is much increased, & by reason of trading being begun to be sett up among us, like to be enlarged more, & the towne being much scattered, whereby many want some sober refreshmt on the Sabbath dayes, upon the motion of Mrs. Anne White we desire to recommend her as a meet [fit] person to the Court, that if they see fitt she may be licensed to keep a house of publicke entertainment."[116] In June 1680, the Salem Court granted Mrs. Anne White a liquor license.[117]

The reason is not given for the *disturbance*. A possible factor may have been associated with Anne's husband Paul. According to Alice Morse Earle in *Stage Coach and Tavern Days*, before he died, Paul was persuaded against his better judgment to open an ordinary (tavern) in 1678. The problem was "he found the occupation so profitable that he finally got into disgrace through it."[118] Paul White, who owned a successful distillery for over 25 years, probably got into the tavern business as a result of the March family problems. The March family owned the Blue Anchor Tavern. The March tavern was located less than a quarter mile from Newbury's meeting

---

[115] Essex County MA, 1912: (vol. 7) 417. NOTE: The court paraphrase and directly quoted the town's petition, hence the need for double quote marks.
[116] Essex County MA, 1912: (vol. 7) 417.
[117] Currier, 1896: 180.
[118] Earle, 1901: 3.

house on the west side of High Street near the head of Marlborough Street. Paul White's house [tavern] was located two houses north of the Blue Anchor Tavern.[119]

In 1678, Hugh March was involved in a court suit about his wife, Dorcas who was found to have a living husband in another state. On August 15, 1678 Hugh March sold his property in Newbury and thus disqualified himself as an innkeeper.[120] This left the town without an ordinary to serve refreshments on Sabbath Day which is why Paul White was asked to open one. Paul White did not have his ordinary license long before he died on July 20, 1679. Marking his grave is one of the earliest gravestones in First Parish Burying Ground. He shares this distinction with Richard Dummer, Sr. and his wife, Frances who also have early type gravestones without art. After Paul's death Anne White inherited the house [tavern] she lived in with her husband. Anne's house and tavern had a sign with a "Bear" on it and may have been known as the "Bear Tavern."[121]

On March 30, 1680 in the Ipswich Court, John March who had taken over the Blue Anchor Tavern from his father Hugh March was granted a liquor and ordinary license.[122] This was two months before the selectmen submitted petitions on Anne White's behalf. The Salem Court gave her a liquor license because they were under the impression that there was no one else in Newbury to operate an ordinary as they cited "Hugh March & his son, John moveing". When in fact, only Hugh March had moved, his son John stayed and reopened the Blue Anchor Tavern. The Newbury selectmen were aware of John March being granted a license yet they claimed the town needed an ordinary to serve liquor on the Sabbath Day. John was only twenty one or twenty two years of age at the time which may or may not have been a factor. In the transcribed court record there is no mention of the March family by the selectmen.

Richard Dummer, Jr., Daniel Pierce, Anthony Somerby, and Peter Cheney were the selectmen who wrote the original two petitions on behalf of Anne White and presented them to the court. These selectmen outright wanted Mrs. Anne White to have this license and did everything in their power to make it happen. This appears to have included manipulation on their part. In their first petition they go so far as to say they want her to be granted a [partial] liquor

---

[119] Currier, 1896: 176-183. Currier has detailed discussion of the location of these two taverns.
[120] Currier, 1896: 177-178.
[121] Essex County MA, 1912: (vol. 8) 419. The reference is to the "sign of the bear".
[122] Currier, 1896: 180.

license until the "next County court at Salem, when her license may be farther enlarged." In the second petition, they conveniently failed to mention that the Blue Anchor Tavern had recently received its license. The selectmen as a group show respect for Mrs. White saying she was capable of handling the license and business of selling liquor. They stood up for her in court.

In June 1680 the Salem Court granted Mrs. Anne White a license to sell wine and liquor in Newbury.[123] The following year on June 28, 1681, Mrs. White "had her former license renewed ….. to draw wine and liquor …"[124] Transcriptions from the Quarterly Court Records show the selectmen of Newbury, who changed every year, came forward on Mrs. White's behalf with a favorable petition for her to be granted a liquor license in subsequent years.[125] As the records became more numerous the transcriptions become shorter. The last record with an explanation is in 1683. It states, "there being much testimony of her suitableness as a tavern keeper at Newbury."[126] The published court records end in 1686. Anne White continued to operate the tavern after 1686. According to historian John J. Currier, Anne White's license was renewed every year for twenty years (1680-1700).[127]

Mrs. Anne White remained a widow until her death in 1706. As a widow she supported herself for twenty years by keeping a tavern and competed with men in the tavern and liquor business. In 1683 in Newbury there were three taverns selling liquor, Hugh March, John March (at Carr's Ferry) and Anne White.[128] Hugh March maintained his license until his death ca. 1693 and the Blue Anchor Tavern was continually operated up until 1716.[129]

Anne White was illiterate as evidenced by the fact she signed her legal documents with an "x".[130] She compensated for this by employing a bookkeeper. On one occasion, she sent her bookkeeper to represent her in a court suit. She was suing a client for non-payment. In that court suit she asked for retribution in the form of "cattle, corn, boards or staves."[131] In other court cases, she hired attorneys to handle matters for her.[132]

---

[123] Currier, 1896: 180.
[124] Essex County MA, 1912: (vol. 8) 127.
[125] Essex County MA, 1912: (vol. 8) 148, 274, 318, (vol. 9) 21, 204, 593.
[126] Essex County MA, 1912: (vol. 9) 21.
[127] Currier, 1896: 180.
[128] Coffin, 1845: 136, 137; Essex County MA, 1912: (vol. 9) 21; Currier, 1902: 443.
[129] Currier, 1896: 187.
[130] Essex County MA, 1912: (vol. 9) 590.
[131] Essex County MA, 1912: (vol. 9) 590.
[132] Essex County MA, 1912: (vol. 9) 441.

Anne White was not the only woman running a tavern. In 1686, 13 people were granted a liquor license in Essex County. Two of those people were women: Mrs. Anne White of Newbury and Sarah Rowell of Amesbury.[133] Six years earlier (1680) a third woman was mentioned as maintaining a tavern in Essex County. In 1680, the Marblehead selectmen petitioned the court on behalf of Elizabeth Elbridges to be granted a liquor license. Because she was a young unmarried woman, the selectmen stated they would watch out for her and assist in preventing any disturbances by the patrons.[134]

❖❖❖❖❖❖❖❖❖❖

---

[133] Essex County MA, 1912: (vol. 9) 593.
[134] Essex County MA, 1912: (vol. 7) 416-417.

At the March 25, 1684 session of the Ipswich Court, Richard Dummer, Jr. and John Pearson were appointed to fix the Newbury [Thurlow's] Bridge on the Bay Road. The court authorized them to hire as many men as necessary. At the September 29, 1685 session, the court again requested that they repair the bridge and promised to pay them at the next session. The delay in the repairs may have been due to reluctance on the part of Dummer and Pearson to advance the necessary money for the repairs. The repairs were eventually completed, and they submitted their bill for expenses at the March 30, 1686 court session.[135]

Beginning in 1680, the General Court began a major reorganization of militia companies. In Newbury they were ordered to divide the militia into two companies of soldiers. These two companies along with other companies from Rowley, Bradford, Andover, Topsfield, Salisbury, Amesbury, and Haverhill were to be formed into a regiment under the Command of Major-General Dennison. The first Newbury company was under the command of Captain Daniel Pierce. The second Newbury Company was commanded by Captain Thomas Noyes.[136] In 1683 Mr. Richard Dummer was appointed by the General Court to be lieutenant of the regiment that Major-General Dennison commanded which included all the towns mentioned above. The following year he is reappointed to a town oriented troop. On February 13, 1684, "The Court, considering that the troope belonging to Newbury & Rowley is not yet compleated with comission officers doe, therefore, appoint, Mr. Richard Dumer captaine, Thomas Lambert, left [Lieutenant], & Henry Short cornet of sd troope."[137] According to historian John J. Currier this third troop was the "cavalry, or mounted dragoons".[138] The military build up was not due to a threat of Indian raids but from an escalating political conflict between the British government and the Massachusetts Bay Colony. This conflict resulted in the colony's charter being revoked in October of 1684.[139]

In a letter, dated August 13, 1687, to Governor Andros from his assistant Robert Mason, Richard is mentioned as being one of two Justices of the Peace in Newbury. Mason was requesting two additional men be named Justice of the Peace. In regards to Richard Dummer, Jr. he writes, "Mr. Dummer the other justice lives six miles from the place and therefore very unfit

---

[135] Essex County MA, 1912: (vol. 9) 217, 533, 593.
[136] Currier, 1902: 497-498.
[137] Shurtleff, 1853: (vol. 5) 431-432.
[138] Currier, 1902: 497.
[139] Currier, 1902: 497.

for the service for the town of Newbury, besides his other qualities in not being of the loyal party as he ought to be."[140] Mason at the time was living in Portsmouth and had reclaimed his father's old land grant. That grant covered all the land between Salem and the Merrimac River. This land conflict had started a few years earlier. The town of Newbury being within those bounds and upset about it had voted back in March 1682, to send Dummer and several other men to court about Mr. Mason's claim.[141] This accounts for Mason's claim that Dummer was no longer a loyal party member. The letter also claims there were no military commissions for Newbury. Mason taking advantage of this situation names the men he wants to see appointed.[142]

In 1688, a tax was levied on all the inhabitants and broken down into several categories. The tax list for Newbury lists "Capt Rich'd Dumer, Esq'r" as owner of 4 houses, 92 acres of land, 3 horses, 2 oxen, 18 cows, 30 sheep and 2 hogs.[143] Many of the upper class, wealthy men owned houses and farms in addition to their home. These additional properties were rented to tenant farmers. In turn, these tenant farms generated an income for the owner.

He and Elizabeth had two more sons, Nathaniel born in 1685 and Shubael born on January 10, 1686/7.[144] He is mentioned one more time before his death. On June 21, 1689 at the meeting held for the election of town officers, Richard Dummer was chosen moderator.[145]

On July 4, 1689, Captain Richard died leaving his wife, Elizabeth, with six children all under the age of fifteen.[146] He was buried next to his father in the First Parish Burying Ground and has a small, light gray colored slate gravestone with artwork by a professional Boston carver. [The gravestone disappeared sometime after this photograph was taken] (Fig. 7) Richard, Jr. like his father was active in public affairs. For him it was county appointments for Newbury town projects and town government. His generation, one removed from the first settlers, had much more local town work than their fathers. The colony's rapid growth relegated more responsibility to the towns out of necessity. Essentially, he followed in his father's footsteps except for the fact he did not have a stone carved to mark his reign on the farm.

---

[140] Currier, 1845: 149.
[141] Coffin, 1845: 136.
[142] Currier, 1902: 195; Coffin, 1845: 149.
[143] Currier, 1902: 202-203.
[144] Watkins, 1969: 20.
[145] Currier, 1902: 208.

Fig. 7 – Richard Dummer, Jr.'s 1689 gravestone in First Parish Burying Ground, Newbury, MA. His headstone was among the very earliest decorated gravestones to make it into Newbury.

---

[146] Watkins, 1969: 20.

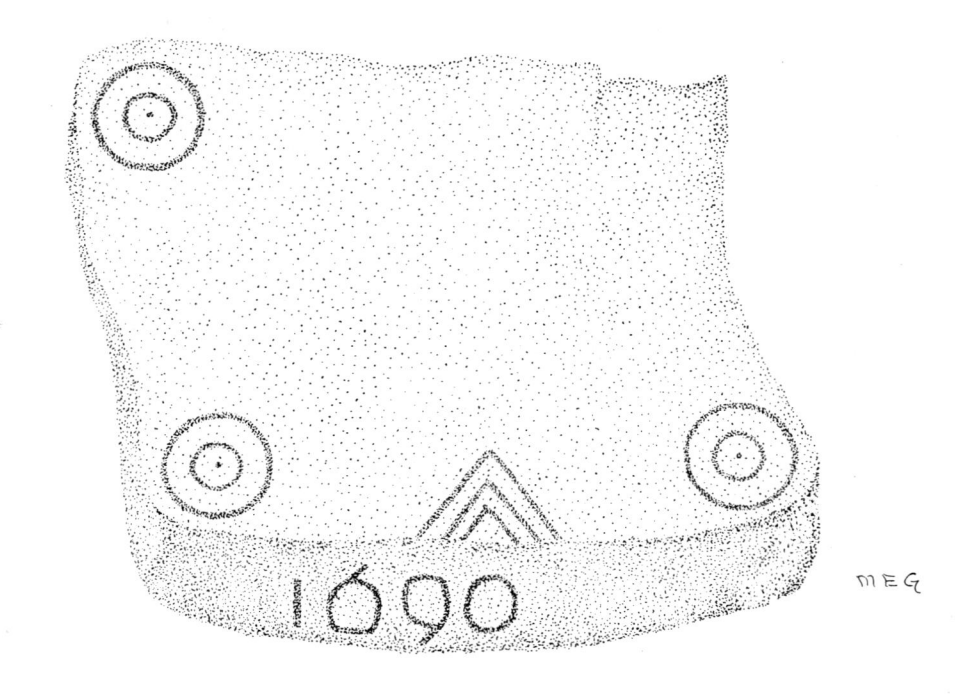

Fig. 8 – 1690 Doorstone. The date "1690" was carved by John Dummer. The circles and triangles were carved by John Hartshorn.
1690 Doorstone is in the collection of the Smithsonian Institution, National Museum of American History. Used with permission.

The Third Generation

A month prior to his death, Richard Jr. had made out a will in which he provided for his wife and children. Elizabeth received her third interest in the property as required by law. John, his eldest son, inherited the part of the farm that included the mansion house, land and a tenant farm. Richard III, nine years old, also received land and a tenant farm. Nathaniel, four years old at the time of his father's death, and Shubael, age 3 were to be paid 100 pounds upon coming of age.[147] Since all his sons were still under age, it meant Elizabeth, their mother, had to manage the farm and tenants for her children.

John Dummer inherited not only the mansion house and land, but the two early doorstones, as well. These carved doorstones greatly impressed the young Dummer, who was only thirteen years old. He undoubtedly had heard stories about his grandfather and the stones, for he knew what they represented. A year later, though not eligible to inherit the farm until he came of age at twenty-one, John nonetheless decided to leave his mark, when he turned fourteen. Fourteen was an age when many boys left home to apprentice with a master craftsman and may have had some significance to him. This is demonstrated by the fact someone, presumably John, crudely carved 1690 on a doorstone, to mark the start of his inheritance (See Fig. 8).[148]

Richard, Jr.'s brother, Jeremiah, who had remained in Boston, also owned land in Newbury (part of the original farm), that he acquired by inheritance and purchase.[149] His property was located on both sides of the country road (Middle Road) and contained a tenant farm. In 1695, Jeremiah gave the land on the west side of the country road to his nephew, Richard, III.[150] This property, with its tenant farmer, was placed in the hands of Elizabeth, Richard's mother, for her support until he came of age. Elizabeth by then had proven she could manage the farm and raise her children. The year Jeremiah deeded the property over to Richard, for her support was just two years short of John inheriting his portion of the farm. Since Richard, III was fifteen years old at the time this gave her six more years of income to assist with the

---

[147] Watkins, 1969: 20.
[148] For a detailed explanation see *The 1690 Doorstone* section.
[149] Watkins, 1969: 22.
[150] Watkins, 1969: 23.

raising of the rest of her children. Two years later on August 8, 1697 John turned twenty-one years old and officially inherited his portion of his father's estate.

John Dummer does not surface in the town history until 1701. This is the year that people from both Newbury and Rowley got actively involved in establishing a new parish. On December 9, 1701 the residents at "The Falls" signed a petition and presented it to the town of Newbury, "Upon ye request of Mrs. Elizabeth Dumer, Mr John Dumer, Mr Joshua Woodman, ... yt the one half of their ministry rate may be abated for the next rate that is to be made."[151] Their request to start a new parish and reduce the tax paid to the town was granted. The inhabitants living at the falls were five miles distant from the First Parish meeting house. The Newbury inhabitants were joined in the creation of this new parish by families who lived in Rowley near [Nelson] Pearson's mills.[152] Women, who had no right to vote in parish, town or colony government, were allowed the right to sign petitions. In this case, Elizabeth was the first person to sign this petition, which suggests she and her son, John may have been the ones to initiate the idea and pursued it. The petition is the last confirmed reference to Elizabeth Dummer in historical records.

About this time in Haverhill, John Hartshorn, a weaver and farmer, had started to carve gravestones.[153] Haverhill is located on the north side of the Merrimac River across from Bradford which bordered both Rowley and Newbury at the time. He was the first carver to make gravestones available to people in the area. For the first seven years, his work was bought by people in his home town and Bradford as well as in Salisbury, MA where he apparently had some contacts.

In 1702, a meeting house was built on the dividing line of Newbury and Rowley by the inhabitants, who had petitioned for a new parish. They then invited Rev. Moses Hale to become their minister and he accepted. John Dummer's sister, Elizabeth married Rev. Moses Hale on January 5, 1704.

The new meeting house needed a parsonage and on April 10, 1703, on an unrecorded deed, John Dummer sold nine acres of his land to the proprietors of the meeting house for a

---

[151] Currier, 1902: 229.
[152] Currier, 1902: 229.
[153] Tucker, 1989: 1.

parsonage. This land for the parsonage house was situated across the street from the church. Later, in June he sold another acre to Rev. Moses Hale.[154]

The next order of business was to give the new parish a name. The parish was first called Rowlbury a combination of the two town's names. Apparently this was not satisfactory and another name was considered. The second choice,

> As the story goes, the name owes its origin to a rivalry between the Sewall and Dummer families. Henry Sewall, the settler, selected his farm along the north side of the river Parker, while Richard Dummer selected his along the south side. Though the families had for generations lived harmoniously, when that section of the town became a parish there was quite a sharp contention between them about the name. Both families claimed the honor of the name, and when the contest was carried into the General Assembly it was finally settled by Judge Byfield, a member, who rose and offered to make the parish a present if they would name it for him. His proposal was at once agreed to and he presented to the church the plate for the communion service and also a bell.[155]

On February 20, 1704 the people of this new parish met and accepted the name "Byfield" in honor of Col. Nathaniel Byfield of Boston.[156]

In 1704, John Dummer married his first wife, Sarah the daughter of Col. Pierce in Newbury. In that same year, his sister, Elizabeth Dummer Hale, sadly died at the age of twenty-two.[157]

At a meeting on October 21, 1706 in Newbury, the boundary lines of the Byfield Parish were established, "... for so long as they shall maintain an orthodox minister amongst them."[158] Rowley followed suit on May 13, 1707. The inhabitants of Byfield Parish now had an authorized, but still unofficial [un-incorporated] parish. The parish had one very pressing issue to deal with. Their meeting house had been built amid a conglomeration of farms without public roads to access it. They addressed this matter during their meeting on June 15, 1708 when it was agreed that, "every man for himself shal and doe grant liberty for a way throw his land for passing to and from meting."[159]

---

[154] Watkins, 1969: 22.
[155] Hurd, 1888: 1717-1718.
[156] Currier, 1902: 229-230.
[157] Watkins, 1969: 22.
[158] Currier, 1902: 230.
[159] Byfield, 1953: 165-166.

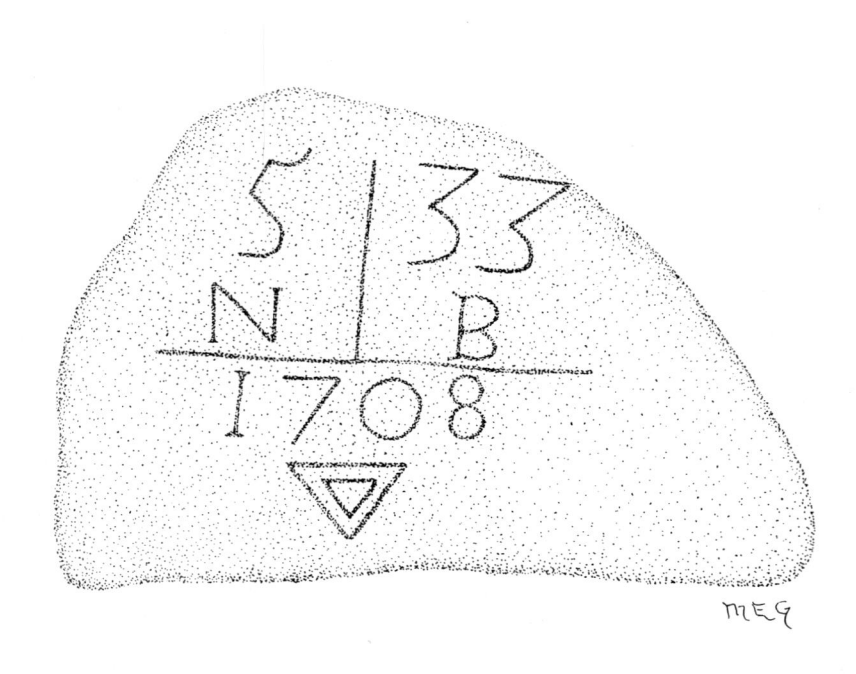

Fig. 9 – Milestone 33 is on the grounds of the Governor Dummer Academy in Byfield, MA. It was carved and erected in 1708 by the local gravestone carver, John Hartshorn.

A few paths were already in existence prior to this date, one of which had previously been opened up and incorporated into the Bay Road. The Bay Road known as the country road was built in the 1660's through Richard Dummer, Sr.'s farm from the Rowley line to Thurlow's bridge where it crossed the River Parker.

Off the section of the Bay Road running through Dummer family lands was a "westerly path," mentioned in a 1695 deed. This was the land Jeremiah Dummer gave to his nephew, Richard Dummer III. The property, given to Richard was bordered on the east by "the country road, viz. the Most westerly path" and on the west by a brook. The brook formed the eastern border of his brother, John's farm.[160] Although there are no maps to show where the "ways" were granted to travel to the meeting house by the inhabitants, it is likely this "westerly path" continued on through John Dummer's farm. For twenty years later, the town purchased land from John Dummer to build a road from the country road (Bay Road) to the meeting house.[161] That road was named Elm Street and although it has been rerouted in the area of the academy and on a small portion near the regional school, it still goes directly to the old Byfield meeting house now a private home.

The opening of these pathways to the public as a means to get to the meeting house, coincided with a gravestone carver traveling through Byfield later that same year. In the latter part of 1708, John Hartshorn, who had become an accomplished carver, left Haverhill after most of his family was killed in an Indian raid in the month of August. From Haverhill he traveled south through Byfield, where his services were called upon to carve the first gravestones for the Byfield Parish.[162] While there, John Dummer hired Hartshorn to carve a milestone and erect it on the Bay Road.

John Dummer was related to Judge Samuel Sewall, who kept close ties with his relatives in Newbury. In 1707, Sewall had two milestones erected in Boston.[163] Mileage from one place to another had been known for the past fifty years. However, there is no evidence that it was marked with any type of signage prior to 1707. Sewall was the first person in the New England colonies to erect milestones giving the mileage to or from a particular place. John undoubtedly

---

[160] Watkins, 1969: 23.
[161] Coffin, 1845: 197.
[162] Tucker, 1989: 1.
[163] Wood, 1919: 147.

learned about the idea from Judge Sewall and then had milestone 33 erected the first one outside of Boston and the third in New England.

In having the milestone carved John was following in his grandfather Richard Dummer, Sr.'s footsteps. He marked an event that was important to him with a carved stone. The event was the establishment of the Byfield Parish. John, however, diverged from his grandfather in one crucial point: he went public with it. This is a noticeable change from earlier Puritan attitudes that would not have allowed it. The milestone was carved with the date 1708, mileage and towns, plus a design (See Fig. 8). The design is a double triangle. The double triangle's symbolism was created by the stone carver and it can be traced back to the design on the 1636 doorstone.

Hartshorn, who had created his own style of artwork on gravestones, had on occasion drawn on pre-existing carved designs for ideas. These he modified to suit his style and imagery. Using this same technique, he created milestone 33 with a similar yet different design from the one found on the 1636 doorstone. This pattern of linking designs from one Dummer stone to another was carried down through the rest of the Dummer stones to come.

Today the milestone stands on the grounds of Governor Dummer Academy at the junction of the old Elm Street and Middle Road. It appears to have always belonged there. However, in 1727, when Elm Street was made, the Lt. Governor's gate was used for a reference marker to the street junction, not the milestone.[164] This is an indication that it may have been moved to its present location at a later date.[165]

John Dummer may also have been making another statement with milestone 33. John was probably the Dummer family member who promoted the Dummer name for the new parish. By erecting the first milestone in Byfield on the country (main) road he publicly gave the Dummer family a presence with a prominent monument in the parish.

Circa 1710 Byfield received its second milestone one mile distant from the Dummer milestone. Milestone 34 was erected on the Sewall side of the River Parker on the country road. It was carved by another carver whose identity is unknown. No connection has been made between this milestone and the Sewall family. However, it is likely they had it erected as a

---

[164] Byfield, 1953: 194.
[165] NOTE: The old Bay Road originally went straight up and over the hill to the Rowley mills. Today it crosses Elm Street and goes up the hill to the apartments for students.

monument on their side of the river. The rivalry between the Dummer family and themselves, over the naming of the parish, suggests this as a likely scenario. No other milestones existed in the town of Newbury until three more were erected twenty years later in the mid 1730's.

John Hartshorn settled down in the town of Rowley. He married again and opened up a gravestone shop there, by 1709.[166] It is at this time that his gravestones begin to appear in the Byfield, Newbury, Rowley and Ipswich burying grounds. Settling in Rowley placed him in an area with neighboring towns that had a fair number of gravestones carved by the professional Boston carvers. This broadened his knowledge of gravestone art, opened him to new ideas, and designs. Some of his most interesting work was done between 1709 and 1710. It was a time when he experimented with designs, concepts and styles.

John Dummer chose the ideal time, when in 1709, he commissioned Hartshorn to carve designs on his own 1690 doorstone (See Fig. 7). Hartshorn incorporated his new thought process and created a design that complemented the 1636 doorstone but set the 1690 doorstone apart. Through the symbolism of the repeated triangle design he connected the 1690 doorstone to the 1708 milestone and to the 1636 doorstone. In addition to the triangles he added a circle repeated inside of itself. However, unlike the 1636 and 1640 doorstones he chose to place the designs on the top surface of the stone where people walk-on instead of on the narrow front side of the stone with the date.

After the parish was established, John Dummer begins to show up as an active member. In 1710, "at this abovsed meting [March 22, 1710] ther were chosen as a comity mr john dumer, john brown & john noyse to inquire into ye paieng of mr hales salery for ye year 1708 of the asesors & colectors, for mr hale demands fourty shilings yt he wants of his salery of yt yeare 1708 & also to se after what have ben over paid in ye yeare 1707, & as soone as they can bring report of what they find to ye company."[167] Later that year, John Dummer signed and sent a petition to the General Court on behalf of the inhabitants of Newbury and Rowley requesting the parish be incorporated. On October 28, 1710 the court granted the incorporation of the Byfield Parish.[168]

---

[166] Tucker, 1989: 1.
[167] Byfield, 1953: 168.
[168] Currier, 1902: 230-231.

Committees of two to three men were usually chosen to deal with transactions and other affairs. An example of this occurred in 1711, when John Dummer and John Brown were asked to procure a bill of sale made out to the Byfield Parish for land purchased by another committee, "for the use of the ministry."[169] Dummer was also chosen to be an assessor that year.[170]

The following year, 1712, John Dummer was chosen as one of the assessors and for another committee. This committee consisted of Mr. John Dummer, Phillip Goodridge and John Smith. Their job was to measure a piece of, "land that cotin frazer laid downe by mr hales house for the conveniency of the pasonag house and way" and lay out another piece of land, equal to it for Cotin Frazer on the south end of the parsonage land.[171] On the Bay Road in south Byfield, yet another land exchange occurred that year. Jeremiah Dummer, who had remained in Boston, owned over four hundred acres in Newbury on the Bay Road in Byfield. On a deed dated November 18, 1712 he gave his son, William [Lt. Governor William Dummer] the land as an outright gift.[172] This land is where the Academy is located today, on Middle Road (Bay Road). William Dummer was John Dummer's cousin.

By 1716, Lt. Governor William Dummer and his wife Catherine were using the Byfield property as a summer residence.[173] Also in 1716, the Lt. Governor asked to build a pew in the Byfield meeting house. The parish decided by a vote, "to grant to his honour our leiutenant governor sir wiliam dummer liberty to buld him a pew in the meting hous, on the front side of the meting hous on which hand do pleas. mr john dumer esquire & deckon moody were chosen to give honour the offer of it."[174] His position as Lt. Governor brought a great deal of respect and added formality to the building of a pew.

Late in 1714, John Dummer officiated at the marriage of Mr. Moody and Ms. Fryer in Essex. He signed another document on November 14, 1718 "John Dummer J. Pec." These two documents confirm he was a justice of the peace but it is not known when he was appointed nor how long he retained the position.[175]

---

[169] Byfield, 1953: 171.
[170] Byfield, 1953: 170-171.
[171] Byfield, 1953: 173-174.
[172] Watkins, 1969: 24.
[173] Phillips, 1945: 47.
[174] Byfield, 1953: 182.
[175] Phillips, 1945: 387.

Around 1714 in Bradford, another weaver by the name of Robert Mullicken, Sr. had taken up gravestone carving. Once Mullicken had mastered the craft, Hartshorn, who had continued to make gravestones for Haverhill and Bradford abruptly stopped. This occurred in 1716.[176] Hartshorn then concentrated on Rowley and Ipswich, while Mullicken's work showed up in Bradford, Haverhill and Newbury. Mr. Mullicken had married a woman from Newbury which gave him a contact with people from that town and an opportunity to pursue his gravestone business there.[177]

Mullicken copied Hartshorn's current style (1715) which he had probably learned from the master carver himself. They were both weavers and undoubtedly knew each other.[178] However, Robert Mullicken's work can be easily distinguished and identified by his non-connected designs in the lunette. Hartshorn in comparison always connected the components in his lunettes with some kind of line.

In 1718, John's brothers, Richard and Nathaniel, begin to show up in the parish records. That year, Nathaniel Dummer was chosen assessor and Richard was chosen as part of a three man committee. The three men were, "impowered to Covenant and agree with mr David Woodman to build an house for the ministre for the fifty seven pounds which the precint has granted for that use."[179] The house being referred to was a large addition to the parsonage.

In 1719, John Hartshorn's fourth wife, Mary Leighton Spofford Hartshorn died.[180] The following year the area's first gravestone carver moved to Norwich, Connecticut where his daughter lived with her husband.[181] Hartshorn was the first and only local gravestone carver for many years. When he arrived in Rowley he readily picked up ideas from the professional Boston gravestones that had made it into the area. From them, he learned to expound upon people's life achievements and express it in words on their stones. He also, became aware of the fact that women were being given equal to or better gravestones than some of the men (See Fig. 10). These two concepts were incorporated into his work and influenced some of his own ideas.

---

[176] Tucker, 1992: 24-25.
[177] Tucker, 1992: 25.
[178] Tucker, 1992: 25.
[179] Byfield, 1953: 183-184.
[180] Tucker, 1989: 1.
[181] Benes, 1986: 161.

Fig. 10 – The elaborate headstone carved by a professional Boston gravestone carver for Ann Chase, dated 1708, is located in Sawyers Hill burying Ground, Newburyport, MA.

The gravestone of Sara Wicom, dated 1705 (carved circa 1708) is an excellent example (See Fig. 20). In the lunette he carved his usual mask like face, but placed a crown on it. He further eulogized Sara with the wording, "A tender mother, A prudent wife, At God command, Aesind [ascend] har [her] Life." On another woman's gravestone (carver unknown but probably Hartshorn), that of Mehetable Moodey, the inscription reads, "Metebale, Dater [daughter] of Mr. Henry & Jane Sewall, wife of Mr. William Moodey Promoted settleng the worship of God here, and then went to her glorified son William, leaueing her son Samuel & four Daters with their Father, August ye 8th, 1702, Aetat 38. "[182] Mehetable was first of all given a gravestone, and secondly she was recognized publicly for helping to establish the Byfield Parish. Her gravestone was replaced in recent years with a new stone that has a modern design. Its original design therefore can not be traced to a specific gravestone carver.

The artwork on gravestones of women, like Sara Wicom, revealed social status. People would have readily recognized her as an important person. Robert Mullicken, Sr., who came after Hartshorn, also learned to use symbolism to denote a person's social status. In 1722, he began to distinguish men with the military rank of Captain from everyone else by carving a skull with wings on their gravestones. In this case, he imitated the professionals to suit his needs and purpose. The skull and wings design, done by the professional carvers, was a common image but only the wealthy could afford the slate gravestones.

When John Dummer decided to have stones carved for his parents in 1723, he went to Robert Mullicken, Sr. Mullicken's work by then was well known in Newbury, Haverhill and Bradford. Not only had he mastered carving but also the art of design and use of symbolism.

John Dummer, who loved carved stones, was intrigued with permanently leaving one's mark. His grandfather, Richard, Sr., had two doorstones, John had the 1690 doorstone and a milestone for the Byfield Parish, but his parents, Captain Richard and Elizabeth did not have any. These stones, however, were to represent two people who had previously reigned on the farm, a break from the norm whereby the stones marked the beginning of a person's reign. For them, he changed to a radical new concept, portrait like images without dates. Another reason for no dates may have been because his mother, Elizabeth never had complete ownership of the farm. The portraitures may also have been influenced by his Uncle Jeremiah's painted portraits. The first was a doorstone carved with an image of a woman and the second a walkway stone with an image of a gentleman (See Fig. 11). The two fitted together as a set of stones at an entrance to the mansion house.

Jeremiah Dummer, the silversmith, also did engraving and painting. There are two portraits by him dated 1691, a self-portrait and another of his wife, Anna. He also painted John Coney and his wife (dated 1708) and is thought to have done the portraits of his son, William, and his wife, Catherine. The first four are signed by him but William and Catherine's which are done in the same style are not signed.[183] Art was a part of the lives of several members of the Dummer family.

---

[182] Jewett & Jewett, 1946: 143.
[183] Phillips, 1945: 38, 41.

Stories Carved in Stone

Fig. 11 – Father's Stone and Mother's Stone

(Top) The Father's stone: A walkway stone carved in 1723 to commemorate Richard Dummer, Jr. Through a symbolic design, the circles with a dot in the middle, this stone is connected to the Mother's stone. The Father's stone is also known as the "Witchstone."

(Bottom) The Mother's stone: A doorstone carved in 1723 to commemorate Elizabeth Dummer. The Mother's stone is in the collection of the Smithsonian Institution, National Museum of American History. Used with permission.

Stories Carved in Stone

The doorstone with the portraiture of woman, the authors have chosen to call "the Mother's stone." It was carved with a woman's face, hearts, fleur-de-lis, circles with a dot in the middle, and the sun. Keeping with the previous theme of linking the Dummer stones via symbols that Hartshorn had started, Mullicken followed suit. He carried over the fleur-de-lis from the 1636 doorstone and the circles from John Dummer's 1690 doorstone.

Elizabeth's stone (i.e. Mother's stone) is a unique piece of carved art. It is a culmination of her importance in John's life and a son's love for his mother. She had finished raising John and his siblings when her husband died. She had kept the farm in operation for seven years, until John came of age, and had managed the tenant farms under her jurisdiction. This gave the family the financial support it needed to keep going and allowed her to remain a widow. Elizabeth was also influential in the establishment of the new parish. Up to that year at least, she had remained a widow for over twelve years, which was an unusually long time for the period. This may have been to protect her underage sons' inheritances from a new husband who by law could take it away.

The book, *The Way of Duty*, brings this fact out in a document composed by Mary Noyes, a widow who was considering getting remarried. In August 1773, she wrote a paper entitled "Portrait of a Good Husband" a part of which included the following, "May he be indeed a father to my fatherless children ... May he look on the inheritance of their deceased father as sacred, never to be converted to his own use or in any way to augment his own estate, ..."[184] It is not known whether or not Elizabeth Dummer ever remarried, nor when she died. A reference in Judge Sewall's diary dated October 8, 1719 states he, "Sat with Madam Dumer and M. Pemerton in her Pue." And "...Rode to Madam Dumer's, and lodg'd there the 4th night." In another entry he states, "and then pass on to the Lieut. Governour's; Bror. Moodey, ..."[185] Sewall makes a clear distinction as to who he is visiting. These passages are therefore highly suggestive of the fact Elizabeth Dummer was probably still living as late as 1719 and had remained a widow. The date, 1723, would put her age at about seventy, not uncommon for a woman who had survived childbearing years.

The authors have chosen to call the stone with the portrait of a gentleman "the Father's stone." The stone has been known locally for many years as the "Witchstone", a reference to the

---
[184] Buel and Buel, 1984: 80.

belief that the geometric designs represented hex symbols. This local name, however, is quite misleading. The Father's stone was the second Dummer stone to be carved by Mullicken (See Fig. 11). It portrays a full figured gentleman, has a single triangle and a symbolic circle in each corner that matches the circles on the Mother's stone. The symbolic circles, which are a modified version of Hartshorn's circles on the 1690 doorstone, were reserved for these two stones.

Like the Mother's stone this stone also has symbolic links. First the triangle forms a direct link with the Dummer family via the 1636 doorstone. Second, the circles with a dot in the middle create a link between two individual people that of a husband and wife, mother and father. In an afterthought, Mullicken ingeniously picked up on this latter link and placed two of the secondary designs (hearts and fleurs-de-lis), from the Mother's stone, on specific gravestones in the town of Newbury. These precisely placed symbols reveal the identity of these two people and the person who ordered the stones.[186] It is the gravestone carver's secret. We rarely think of these early generations as having a sense of humor or expressing a joke. Yet this inside story per se is just that as it was not meant for public viewing or acknowledgement.

At the March 3, 1723/4 meeting, "Leiut Nathaniel Dummer, Decon Daniel Jewett & mr. Thomas Coleman were chosen to consider what maner of house to build as to the form & Demention and what the expences of sd meeting house may amount unto and make return to the Precinct."[187] The following January 25, 1724/5 Mr. Richard Dummer along with Deacon Wm. Moody, Leiut. Spaford and two others were chosen for a committee to build the addition on the west end of the meeting house.[188] All three of the Dummer men living in Byfield from the third generation were actively involved in parish affairs. There is a pattern to the public activities of the Dummer men who chose to live in Newbury. The first generation, Richard, Sr. starts out in the General Court in Boston where all colony business was initially conducted. As the colony grew it began to reallocate its business to local towns and district courts to take on more of the work load. In following Richard, Sr.'s public career we see how his positions shift from Boston to county government and a couple of town positions. When his son, Richard, Jr. starts

---
[185] Ewell, 1904: 81.
[186] For a detailed explanation see *The Mother Stone* section.
[187] Byfield, 1953: 189.
[188] Byfield, 1953: 190.

participating in public affairs his positions are town oriented with the exception of the military appointments. The third generation comes of age with the opening of the Byfield parish and subsequently all their public work is centered inside the new parish. In comparison are their Boston cousins, William and Jeremiah, Jr. sons of Jeremiah. Jeremiah Sr. was wealthy, well known and well connected, as well as an important person in upper class society. Two of his sons reflect their father's position: Jeremiah, Jr. was Massachusetts Bay's and later Connecticut's agent in England for many years and his more famous brother, William became Lt. Governor of Massachusetts. Interestingly, both of these brothers were instrumental in initiating new schools. While agent for Connecticut Jeremiah, Jr. persuaded Elihu Yale to donate his books to the Connecticut College which resulted in the school being called Yale. Lt. Gov. William being childless set up a trust for his Newbury estate, the large acreage of land and mansion house, to be turned into a school that became the Governor Dummer Academy.[189] Nathaniel of the third generation in Newbury was one of the overseers of this school when it was first established. John Dummer's farm the former home of Richard Dummer, Sr. through no connection with either man ironically became the site of Triton Regional School.

As the parish grew, they reached a point where there were enough families to support a school and a teacher within the boundaries of the parish. In their meeting on March 7th they chose a committee of three including Lieut. Nathaniel Dummer, to petition their respective towns to exempt the parish from paying taxes to support the town schools.[190] In that same year, 1727, the town of Newbury, laid out a road (Elm Street) two rods wide, "from ye country road near to his honor the lieutenant governor Dummer's house to the parsonage land in Byfield parish on the land of John Dummer esquire, Mr. Richard Dummer and Mr. Joseph Noyes."[191] Byfield from its incorporation grew fairly rapidly and like Newbury proper was concerned with their children's education. They also, sought out the support of the town to build roads for them which shifted the expense from the parish to the town.

Over in Bradford, Robert Mullicken, Sr. had continued to carve gravestones until 1727. However, he was not alone in the shop, his sons Robert, Jr. and John Mullicken had also taken

---

[189] Phillips, 1945: (vol. 81) 41-42.
[190] Byfield, 1953: 194.
[191] Coffin, 1845: 197.

up the trade. They gradually took over completely and took on their younger brother, Joseph as an apprentice about 1729.

Lt. Governor William Dummer, from the year he built his house in Byfield, spent his summers there, where he attended and generously supported the parish. During the Colonial era it was common practice for men of wealth to give their churches a gift of silver.[192] In 1729, he gave the Byfield church two silver communion cups, engraved with his coat of arms and inscribed as follows:[193]

<blockquote>
DEDICATED
BY WM. DUMMER, Esqr.,
TO THE CHURCH OF
NEWBURY FALLS,
FOR THE
COMMUNION TABLE,
1729
</blockquote>

It is interesting to note the name by which he calls the church. Byfield Parish was composed of two towns Rowley and Newbury. Occasionally it was necessary to distinguish one side from the other. When this happened the Newbury side was referred to as, "the people at the falls." A fire burned the church in 1833, but the two the silver communion cups survived.[194] These two silver communion cups are in the Museum of Fine Arts, Boston, Massachusetts.

Like many towns, parishes experienced growing pains. On July 14, 1730, John Dummer, Esq., Mr. Ebenzer Stuert and Lieut. Stephen Longfellow were chosen to go to the General Court in Boston, "to answer to a petion put in to said Cort by the wasterly [westerly] part of Rowly and sum of byfild parish."[195] At the March 1, 1730/1 meeting there were two articles that showed there was some dispute with the Rowley people. Nathaniel Dummer and two others were chosen to arrange an exchange of some families from the old parish of Rowley with the Byfield parish. Then at the May meeting 1731 Mr. E. Stuart was sent back to the General Court in Boston to settle the matter. Also, at that meeting, it was voted that the meeting house would forever be

---

[192] Bigelow, 1917: 394.
[193] Dummer, 1888: 28.
[194] Dummer, 1888: 28.
[195] Byfield, 1953: 256.

located on the line between Rowley and Newbury. At the November meeting, a committee of five men including Lieut. Nathaniel Dummer were chosen to, "sate [set] the meeting house Rule for satting by age & rates."[196]

About 1730, William Dummer retired from government. From that year on it is known he lived in Byfield, at least part of the year, where he maintained a pew in the meeting house.[197] He also, kept his School Street home in Boston where he periodically returned to.[198] Richard Dummer, III had moved to Rowley with his wife, who came from that town.[199] John Dummer, remained at the original mansion house his grandfather, Richard Dummer, Sr. had built. He went on to marry four times, before he had any children. His second wife was Mrs. Mercy Gardner of Haverhill, the third wife was a daughter of Hon. Samuel Penhallow and the fourth was Mrs. Elizabeth Dummer.[200] He and his fourth wife, Elizabeth, had their first child, a daughter, Katharine on May 8, 1731 and a son, John, born on August 8, 1733.[201]

Nathaniel Dummer continued to live on the part of the farm given to him by his brother, John, in lieu of the one hundred pounds inheritance owed to him upon coming of age. Nathaniel had not received any land in his father's will but was provided for.[202]

In a continued effort to accommodate the influx of people into the parish, at the March 1732/3 meeting, Nathaniel Dummer and Mr. Joseph Noyes were asked to petition the outer parishes of Newbury to settle on boundary lines with the Byfield Parish.[203] This eventually evolved in the establishment of a new parish that became part of the town of Georgetown.

At this time Newbury's centennial was close at hand, and John Dummer, Esq. of Byfield decided to give the town a gift. As usual, he chose carved stones and called upon the services of Robert Mullicken, Sr., who was now in his sixties. Dummer ordered three milestones to be erected between Byfield and First Parish. These like the other two stones Mullicken had carved for Dummer are undated and not mentioned in the written records.

---

[196] Byfield, 1953: 256-258.
[197] Watkins, 1969: 24.
[198] Phillips, 1945: 48.
[199] Watkins, 1969: 23.
[200] Newbury, 1911: 587.
[201] Watkins, 1969: 23.
[202] Watkins, 1969: 27.
[203] Byfield, 1953: 260.

The gift of the milestones may have come about as a friendly rivalry with his cousin the Lt. Governor. Only six years earlier, William had given the church communion silver inscribed with his coat-of-arms. Both of these public gifts showcased the Dummer family's wealth and social position in Byfield.

Dummer's original 1708 milestone in Byfield reads "N 5" Newbury five miles and "B 33" Boston thirty-three miles. Mullicken's job was to carve three milestones, decorated with geometric designs, for miles 35, 36 and 37 (See Figs. 12, 13 & 14).[204] This brought the milestones outside of Byfield and into First Parish, but short of the port at the mouth of the Merrimac River.

Milestone 37 like milestone 33 is distinctly marked with a double triangle that indicated the end of the series of milestones. However, mile 39 which was within the boundaries of Newbury until the 1760's would have been a more logical choice for ending the series. It would have marked all of the miles on the Bay road between the Rowley-Newbury town line and the Newbury-Salisbury line. John Dummer's decision to end the series of milestones at mile 37 appears to be a deliberate choice.

The town of Newbury was made up of two distinct geographical areas. At the north side of town was the mouth of the Merrimac River that offered a good protected harbor and to the south and west were the rich alluvial soils which provided fertile agricultural fields. By the early 1700's, some of Newbury's residents were creating a large coastal and international trade business along with a substantial ship building business along the Merrimac River. Between 1697 and 1714, over 100 ships were registered in the port of Newbury.[205] These new merchant businesses brought an influx of new wealth which came into the hands of the sea captains and ship owners. This new wealth created a new emerging and predominately American social class known as the mercantile elite.[206]

---

[204] Mile 34 was originally marked by a milestone carved circa 1710 by an unknown carver. At some point this milestone was badly damaged and used as building material in a nearby stone wall. This leaves open the possibility that John Dummer had milestone 34 replaced with one carved by the Mullickens.
[205] Currier, 1902: 480.
[206] Beaudry, n.d.: 2.

Fig. 12 – Milestone 35 on Middle Road, Newbury, MA. Carved circa 1735.

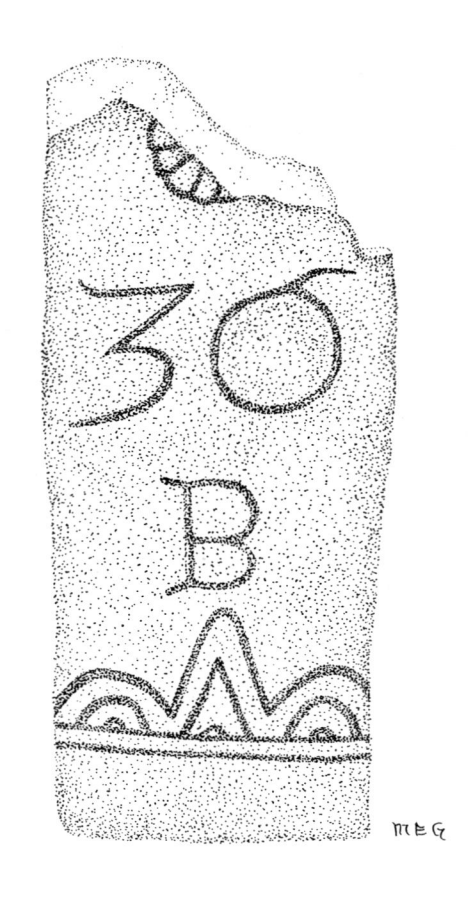

Fig. 13 – Milestone 36 on Boston Road, Newbury, MA. Carved circa 1735.

Fig. 14 – Milestone 37 on Green Street, Newbury, MA. Carved circa 1735.

This new social class began to clash both socially and politically with the farm families like the Dummers who adhered to the old British class system. The British class system embodied such notions that land was the basis of wealth and power, that agriculture was the only honorable business to engage in and a three tier class structure of the rich aristocracy, the artisans, and the working poor. For the mercantile elite, money became the basis of wealth and power and international trade the preferred business.[207] In 1763, the port section of Newbury petitioned to be set off as a separate town and cited as one of its reasons according to historian, J. J. Currier, "Considerable emphasis was laid upon the fact that the farming population persistently opposed any and all measures advocated by 'the merchants, traders, and mechanics living at the waterside'."[208]

Miles 38 and 39 fell in the heart of the port section of town. In ending the series of milestones at mile 37, Dummer was marking a social and political boundary between the merchant elite of the port and the farm families.

Mullicken accepted the job, but chose to enlist the help of his three adult sons. The project became a family affair very much like the way the gravestone shop was operated. It was not uncommon for one of the Mullickens to do the artwork and another to do the lettering on the same gravestone. Likewise, an apprentice's work was often incorporated on the gravestones carved by the masters. Individualism was accepted and possibly encouraged, like creating one's own style of artwork, however, no one stood out as being more important or better.

Of the four Mullickens, Robert, Sr., Robert, Jr. and John were master craftsmen, Joseph was an apprentice. Two of them, Robert, Sr. and John carved an individual milestone. The third and final milestone was carved by all four members of the Mullicken family. This appears to have been done to allow Joseph to participate in this prestigious and historic project.

Milestones by then were fairly common, judging by the four towns south of Newbury, who had quite a number of them. Of the many miles that were marked, only one had a stone that stood out. In Wenham, the 20th mile happened to be directly in front of the meeting house and burying ground. This prompted an unknown person to have it carved with,

JOB THE 30 23

---

[207] Beaudry, n.d.: 5.
[208] Currier, 1902: 266.

Stories Carved in Stone

> I KNOW THAT THO
> WILT BRING ME
> TO DEATH AND TO
> THE HOUSE ~
> APPOINTED FOR
> ALL LIVING
> ### 1710

Undoubtedly this milestone was once well known and recognized for its appropriate saying. It embodied the "living" people who attended the meeting and the "dead" who were buried beside the church.

The Mullickens had a similar job of making their milestones standout. It is through the use of large letters and bold designs that the Mullickens achieved this. The artwork also served a secondary role of identifying the family who had ordered these milestones. Each milestone has a unique design but one that emulates previous Dummer stones. It is the artwork which links all of the stones together. Robert Sr. understood this when he had the double triangle carved on milestone 37. The triangle design which had originated on the 1636 doorstone was used in various forms on the 1690 doorstone, the Mother's stone and Father's stone, the 1708 milestone, and finally on milestone 37.[209]

In the case of the milestones, the gravestone carvers worked with John to make a public statement distinguishing between farm and port. In doing so they created a very private inside story that although viewed by the general public remained a secret. When the Dummer milestones are compared to the milestone in front of the meeting house with its odd verse one has to wonder if a lot more of these types of puzzles were popular. Robert Mullicken had previously created a puzzle by use of symbolism on his gravestones indicating who the people were on the Mother's stone and Father's stone. He knew exactly how to do it. Puzzle mugs and jugs, with oddly placed holes in their sides, were imported from England from the 1600's up to 1750. Elizabeth Stillinger states, "Another popular item was the puzzle jug, in whose neck holes were cut to give rise to such challenges as,

Here, gentlemen, come try your skill

---
[209] See individual stones for a detailed explanation.

Stories Carved in Stone

> I'll hold a wager if you will,
> That you drink not this liquor all,
> Without you spill or let some fall."[210]

The Englishmen of the seventeenth and eighteenth did indeed have a sense of humor some of which appears to have filtered into the Puritan based Mass Bay Colony.

John Dummer, who ordered these milestones, died July 19, 1735, one hundred years after his grandfather had first settled in Newbury.[211] He is buried in Byfield's old burying ground next to the brick meeting house which is now a private residence. His gravestone was carved by Richard Leighton of Rowley, a descendant of the Hartshorn line of gravestone carvers.

One of the legacy's of John Dummer, of the third generation, is the prolific number of carved stones. He had seven in all done. Their symbolically carved art, so ingeniously brought down from the first generation, through the third generation, reveals the Dummer family's story. It gives us a little insight into one family's life, what was important to them, and what they tried to protect. The final milestone with its double triangle marks the end of an era.

Fig. 15 – John Dummer's gravestone in the Byfield Burying Ground on Elm Street, Byfield, MA.

---

[210] Stillinger, 1973: 91, 131.
[211] Watkins, 1969: 23.

The Merrimac Valley Gravestone Carvers

Fig. 16 – Sara Safford's 1712 headstone carved by John Hartshorn. It shows the Merrimac Valley Style with its mask like faced and circle designs beside the face. It is in Ipswich, MA.

Fig. 17 – Example of a professional Boston carved gravestone with skull and wing design. Tristram Coffin's 1703/4 in the First Parish burying Ground, Newbury, MA.

Introduction

...New England gravestone makers energetically and watchfully developed the craft into what has been acknowledged as the highest state of the art attained in the American colonies." [212]

Beginning in the 1670's, a new trend emerged amongst the wealthy fueled by the availability for the first time in the Massachusetts Bay Colony by craftsman skilled in the art of gravestone making. For those who could afford it, gravestones became preferable to the wooden grave markers. Gravestones offered a permanent and lasting monument to the deceased person and a means for the upper class to show off their wealth, an action otherwise forbidden in Puritan New England. For the first twenty five years these were professionally carved stones from Boston and Charleston. They started out with stark death and afterlife symbolic designs which transitioned to the skull and wing design that became the industry standard. Starting in Boston they spread out to coastal port towns where the gravestone phenomenon was accompanied by itinerant stonecutters as was the case in Newbury. By 1700, the first of many rural carvers began plying the trade in Haverhill, Massachusetts. These rural stonecutters, local men of the community, whose ability ranged from poor to excellent were patronized by their hometowns and nearby towns where they had relatives, friends or were generally well known. In some cases theirs were the only stones to be found in the burying grounds whereas along the coast their stones were mixed in with the professionals.

By today's standards rural carver's designs are peculiar and strange images. In Haverhill, John Hartshorn created a simple oval face with geometric type features. A design so well accepted in Haverhill and neighboring Bradford that local patrons shunned the skull and wings as evidenced by the fact that only two stones of this design were carved by the local carvers, both stones were for militia Captains. This persisted until the third generation of rural stone carvers started carving skulls in the mid 1730's.

Gravestone carvers were craftsmen, as well as artists, whose canvas was the gravestone. On many stones the secondary designs found are non-symbolic in nature indicating the carvers had some artistic liberty beyond death/afterlife symbolism. To obtain ideas for designs, they learned from each other and borrowed from many sources including everyday household items.

---
[212] Benes, 1977: 13.

These designs were then expounded and expanded upon transitioning them in different ways. Beginning circa 1700, both the professional and rural carvers restricted by the fact they had to use standard primary designs, skull and wings or oval head, began to have a great deal of freedom in their secondary designs. They were no longer forced to the use of vine and fruit in the side border design. This is seen in both the professional and rural carvers work on the north shore of Boston. Many of these secondary designs are found on furniture, ceramics, glass, and silver which were both made in the colony and imported.

From the beginning, ministers fought a losing battle against a people who for the most part immigrated to the colony for land and business purposes rather than religious. These were the upper and middle class people accustomed to the finer things in life, including art. This art made it into the home in the form of decorative art on furniture and other items, where it could not be controlled. When comparing decorative art on household items to gravestone art, almost every kind of design found on gravestones can be found on ceramics, furniture or silver. This includes geometric designs, flowers, vines, stars, crosshatching borders, caricatures, birds, winged cherubs and portraits (post 1725). The winged cherub shows up on a late seventeenth century ceramic covered tankard by John Dwight of Fulham, England.[213] It was used along with a bust of a gentleman, perched birds, flying birds, a common man walking, flower heads and flowers attached to stems with leaves. The winged cherub in use here has nothing to do with death or afterlife, it is merely decoration. However, it is easy to see how such a whimsical angelic design was converted to an accepted symbolic design on gravestones. Yet on the same tankard are seen geometric styled flower-heads without stems or leaves floating in empty space that also show up in finials of gravestones. The flower-head is transferred to the gravestone but not converted to a symbolic design it remains a simple common everyday design.

This use of common non-symbolic designs came about over a period years. Professional gravestone art started out with skeletons (death itself) and hourglasses (represents time is running out), transitioned to skull and wings with fruit and vines, then went to skull and wings with abstract non-representational side border designs and last to a cherub with wings often surrounded with cheerful flowers. The rural carvers of the Merrimac Valley Style started out with an oval face and what appear to be primitive wings. Those wings developed into an abstract

---

[212] Benes, 1977: ???.

design of bars interspersed with circled geometric designs. Side borders started out as facsimiles of the professional fruit and vine, transitioned to an abstract design with a form of fleur-de-lis, and then to a leafed vine. The second carver upon entering the business in 1714 left out the early wings and bars and changed over to common designs like hearts and fleur-de-lis beside the oval face. Designs not normally associated with death and gravestones. He quickly transitioned to non-symbolic circled geometric designs and what appear to be stars, as fillers in the lunette, which are later dropped in lieu of a stylized flower and other abstract designs. His side borders are mainly a non-descript spiral design. Both use an hour glass on some of their footstones. The use of non-symbolic designs by both professional and rural carvers is another reflection of changes taking place in society.

The cherub introduced by the professionals was not accepted by everyone therefore the skull and wings remained in used until a complete changeover took place with the urn and willow around 1800. By comparison the rural carvers of the Merrimac Valley Style consciously started out with non-death symbolism and geometric designs. This was maintained up until 1738 when a shift comes about in the form of a non-winged skull, by what is considered the third generation carvers of Bradford. This wingless skull was possibly brought about by the distemper epidemic. In the mid 1740's, this third generation style develops wings and eventually shifts to strange caricatures similar to the face designs being used in southern Massachusetts.

In the process a highly specialized folk art form emerged governed not by symbolism but by local patrons based on what they would or would not accept. John Hartshorn's simple oval face that was carried on by his predecessors with many varying secondary designs became known as the Merrimac Valley Style (See Fig. 16).[214] The Merrimac Valley Style was part of a much larger shift in the arts. As early as the 1670's, there was a subtle shift in social thinking away from the strict Calvinist values of the Puritan ministers toward the more enlightened European social trends. Between 1690 and 1700 this shift becomes quite evident in the decorative arts. Art emerges from the privacy of the home into the public sphere as illustrated by the beautifully carved gravestones in the burying grounds, the fancy clothing, and even the ornate silver communion sets in the meeting houses. From 1690 onward, decorative art becomes more common and shows a newly found expressive freedom as craftsmen develop new designs and

---

[213] Stillinger, 1973: 35.

styles. In colonial New England, these changes are marked by the development of definable art movements like the Merrimac Valley Style.

From 1700 to 1725, John Hartshorn, Haverhill's first local carver and his predecessor, Robert Mullicken, Sr. from Bradford had very few examples to show them the way. In creating their works of art they experimented both with designs and how to apply them. At first everyone got a similar stone irregardless of rank or social status in the community. As the two men got to view other burying grounds that had professionally carved stones their ideas broadened. It was during this same period of time, the professionals had found a market in Ipswich and Newbury for their new cherub face with wings, carved on larger more elaborately decorated gravestones. These are the same towns patronized by the two rural carvers.

Influenced by these outside forces, changes are seen in the two rural carvers' work. Those changes reflect what the rural carvers felt was important, for they were the ones who chose the design on the gravestone and how to use it. From the professionals they picked up on how to set a person they felt was important locally, apart from the rest of the people buried in the burying ground. This may also be where they were introduced to crossbones and the hourglass. These death symbols were used by the rural carver's on footstones, but not on their headstones.

Gravestone carvers whether professional or rural found it necessary to work within the confines of accepted designs and styles. This challenged them to stretch their minds to find ways in which their individuality could show through. In doing so, each one developed, perhaps unbeknown to themselves, a signature. That "signature" like a person's hand written signature was unique and maintained for the duration of his career, showing up even within various changes of design over the years. It identifies a carver's work and allows it to be traced. An example of how this works can be seen when Robert Mullicken, Jr. and his brother, John's gravestones are compared to each other. Robert, Jr. favored a tall, separated, two piece design under the face and crescent shaped whorls, whereas John favored a low, spread out design under the face and fan-shaped whorls.

One of the interesting features of both Hartshorn's and the Mullicken family's gravestones were that no two gravestones are exactly alike. This was achieved mainly through different secondary designs. No gravestone design remained the same, throughout its use minor

---

[214] Tucker, 1989: 3-5.

changes were always being made. No two gravestone carvers in this study made identical types of stones. The carvers in this study in their artistic and creative quest, created an individual identity for themselves and individual stones for each deceased person.

What gave gravestone carvers their own personal identity reiterated itself in the decorative utilitarian stones. John Hartshorn and Robert Mullicken, Sr., the two main carvers, were first and second in their trade. When they started out, they did not have any standards or preconceived ideas and ended up developing their own. In turn, ordinary designs could and did occasionally take on symbolic significance. In the following pages, an overview highlights the development of each carver's artwork. It allows a brief look at how the designs they created and used on the gravestones carried over to Dummer's doorstones and Newbury's milestones.

John Hartshorn (1650 - 1738)

Carved:

1690 Doorstone (1 of 2 carvers who worked on this stone)

1708 Milestone

John Hartshorn, in his early twenties, settled in Haverhill where he purchased a farm in 1672. Another brother had also, settled there, where their father, Thomas Hartshorn owned land. Their father was then living in Reading with his wife, Sarah, formerly the "widow Lamson" of Ipswich. When Sarah married Thomas, she brought along her young son, Joseph. Joseph Lamson, John's stepbrother, became the colony's leading gravestone carver in Charlestown where he setup his shop in 1680.[215]

John was a farmer, soldier, and weaver before he took on the gravestone trade. He served in King Philip's War and he also served as a lieutenant in the Haverhill militia. Later in life, he moved to Norwich, Connecticut. In a journal kept by John's nephew-in-law, Joshua Hempstead of Connecticut, there are several entries mentioning gravestones and wool by the pound. Joshua was partially paying John in wool for gravestones he bought from him. Later as Joshua received orders, he lettered the gravestones previously carved with artwork and resold them.[216]

In the early 1700's Hartshorn began carving very simple gravestones, at age fifty.[217] When his earliest work is compared with the common field stone markers, done by the unskilled hand, it shows he had some basic knowledge. His stones are shaped and have a clean, flat finish with simple geometric designs in the side borders and a simple face with curved radiating lines, like wings, in the lunette (See Fig. 18). The lettering is neat and evenly spaced with appropriate words.

---

[215] Benes, 1973: 160-61.
[216] Benes, 1973: 161-162.
[217] Tucker, 1989: 3.

Stories Carved in Stone

Fig. 18 – This is a very early example of John Hartshorn's gravestones. Elizabeth ---- carved circa 1703 in the Pentucket Burying Ground, Haverhill, MA.

Fig. 19 – Hasel Elpony's 1714 Headstone shows Hartshorn's mask like face with the decorative segmented lines he developed, geometric pie shaped finials and side borders with a modified Boston design. It is located in the Ipswich Burying Ground, Ipswich, MA.

His oval mask like face has become the distinguishing characteristic of the Merrimac Valley Style which Hartshorn created.[218] This established his identity and style. Along with his mask like face, he eventually developed intricate geometric designs, some original and others modified from professional designs (See Fig. 19).

John Hartshorn's gravestones first appeared in Haverhill and Bradford. His work was purchased mainly by these two towns until 1708, except for a few stones that made it into Salisbury and North Andover, MA.[219] In that year, as his gravestone carving picked up, Indians made a raid on Haverhill attacking and killing people in several families. During the raid, on August 29th, Hartshorn's wife, Joanna, his oldest son and three grandchildren were killed.[220] After this tragic event he left Haverhill and moved southward passing through Byfield to Rowley.

In Byfield there is an example of his early 1708 style design on Elizabeth Hale's gravestone. There is also another example of a later style design from 1708 on the gravestone of Joshuah Woodman, Jr. (died 1706). Joshuah Woodman Jr.'s is a transitional design with wide plain curving bars last used in the year 1708 before he changed to the segmented version seen on Mr. Joshuah Woodman's stone (died 1703). These gravestones show he had contact with the residents of Byfield in 1708 and his relocation to Rowley 1708/9 meant he had to travel south through the parish to get there. That placed Hartshorn in Byfield in 1708 the year carved on milestone 33 (See Fig. 9).[221]

This was followed by his gravestones showing up in Rowley. One of the earliest in Rowley was a stone, dated 1705 (carved circa 1708), for Sara Wicom, the wife of Daniel Wicom Jr. (Fig. 20). On her stone, Hartshorn carved a crown on top of the face and an elaborate bell side border. Sara's gravestone appears to be the first one Hartshorn carved for the Rowley Burying Ground and in doing so, he made it compliment her father-in-law, Captain Daniel Wicom's 1700 professionally carved gravestone (Fig. 21). Captain Daniel's gravestone and one other are the only two left that date prior to Hartshorn's arrival in Rowley. However, there were at least two other gravestones erected before 1700, the first was for a woman, Elizabeth Pickard,

---

[218] Tucker, 1989: 1.
[219] Slater, Tucker, Farber, 1978: 137.
[220] Tucker, 1989: 1.
[221] See 1708 milestone for a detailed explanation.

Fig. 20 – Sara Wicom's gravestone, dated 1705 is a fine example of John Hartshorn's work to create artwork on a gravestone to compliment the Boston carvers' work. In addition, this gravestone exemplifies a woman's high social status. Rowley Burying Ground, Rowley, MA.

Fig. 21 – Captain Daniel Wicom's Boston made headstone in the Rowley Burying Ground, Rowley, MA. This is one of several early carved stones in this cemetery.

dated 1686. The second was for Captain Moses Bradstreet, dated 1690.[222] These gravestones undoubtedly stood out amongst the common wooden markers used for the rest of the people buried there.

The basic style on Sara's stone was being used by Hartshorn when he arrived in Rowley. However, the artwork on her stone appears to be an evolution of an earlier design that culminated in a crown, acknowledging Sara's high social status. Also, her stone appears to be the first one Hartshorn did to accompany a professional's stone which probably further influenced its creation. Hartshorn, who was influenced by the impressive examples done by the professionals, did not copy their work. What he did was modify their ideas to suit his thoughts and needs.

In 1709, Hartshorn's gravestones begin to appear in Newbury's two burying grounds. By then, Newbury had several slate gravestones and one slab-top tombstone in the First Parish burying ground. The slate gravestones with elaborate designs interestingly were of equal quality, for both men and woman. The 1704 slab-top tombstone was of a completely different type of stone and style. It is the size of the coffin and lies flush with the ground. The impressive stone was carved with two distinct fleurs-de-lis in the top corners (See Fig. 22). The symbolic fleur-de-lis denote a man of importance, in this case, Colonel Pierce.

These Boston gravestones in Newbury further influenced Hartshorn's work. An excellent example is the gravestone he carved for Mary Sawyer, who appears to be the first *Sawyer* buried in Sawyers Hill Burying Ground. (The burying ground although named after the Sawyer family was public and used by the Second Parish of Newbury.) For her headstone he used his most up-to date design, with an extra fancy side border, and on the footstone a completely new concept. For her footstone Hartshorn used Colonel Pierce's tombstone as his example.

Hartshorn picked up on the use of symbolism to denote social status and carved it on Mary Sawyer's footstone. Mary's unusual footstone is identical to the Colonel's tombstone (except in size). It has a fleur-de-lis in each of the top corners and a rectangular shape like the tombstone (See Fig. 23). This shows a radical change and sophistication in his thought process. Mary Baily's footstone and headstone, also in Sawyer's Hill and dated 1708, is an example of his

---

[222] Jewett & Jewett, 1946: 141.

Stories Carved in Stone

Fig. 22 – One of two fleur-de-lis on Colonel Pierce's 1704 slab-top tombstone in First Parish Burying Ground, Newbury, MA.

Fig. 23 – One of two fleur-de-lis on Mary Sawyer's 1708 footstone by John Hartshorn copied from Colonel Pierce's tombstone. Her footstone is in Sawyer's Hill Burying Ground, Newburyport, MA.

Stories Carved in Stone

Fig. 24 – Mary Bailey's 1708 standard type footstone for this time period by John Hartshorn. Sawyer's Hill Burying Ground, Newburyport, MA.

Fig. 25 – Mary Sawyer's 1708 headstone carved by John Hartshorn with fancy artwork that sets her apart from her contemporaries. Sawyer's Hill Burying Ground, Newburyport, MA.

conventional style in use at the time (See Fig. 24). He clearly distinguishes between the two women showcasing the woman who he saw as important through elaborate public art.

Mary Sawyer's headstone shows the same elaborate, sophisticated thought process as her footstone. It has a very fancy, one of a kind scroll in the side border that ends with hearts.[223] In the lunette, Hartshorn used curved segmented lines his newest, most sophisticated design rather than the crown he used on Sara Wicom's stone. The artwork accorded to Mary Sawyer, placed her in an elite class by herself, above every man and woman buried in Sawyer's Hill (See Fig. 25). The combination of artwork on both her footstone and headstone indicate it was carved circa 1709.

In Sawyers Hill Burying Ground there is another gravestone dated 1708 for Ann Chase, wife of Ensign Moses Chase (See Fig. 10). Her headstone, carved by a professional Boston carver, is elaborately decorated with two winged skulls, fancy side border designs and beautiful lettering. Not only does it standout among others for its time, it is of a finer quality than most gravestones done for men. It is impossible to ascertain which gravestone was erected first Ann Chase's or Mary Sawyer's. What is of interest is these gravestone carvers, of which all were men, went to great lengths to provide high quality gravestones for these women. Albeit these were special cases, they still represent an unusual social attitude toward women. Furthermore, it should be noted the husband or family of these women opted for the extra cost of providing a stone verses a wooden marker.

In 1709, Hartshorn settled in Rowley and married Mary Spofford.[224] On his gravestones that year, he makes three significant changes. The first shows up in connection with the circled designs of rosettes, whorls, etc. He encircled the designs with a plain band. A style he used for the remainder of the time he was in Rowley. The second change involved adding circled designs next to the mask like face in the lunette on some of his gravestones (See Fig. 26). The final change, which completed the transition, was replacement of the narrow and wide bar curved lines with segmented lines (See Fig. 75). These changes are important for they were used as a guide to date his gravestones, when he moved from Haverhill to Rowley. This also, aided in dating the designs he carved on John Dummer's 1690 doorstone. The gravestones from the

---

[223] Slater, Tucker, Farber, 1978: 128.
[224] Tucker, 1992: 25.

Fig. 26 – Ensign Henry Lunt's 1709 headstone with its circle designs placed in the lunette beside the face. It is located in the First Parish Burying Ground, Newbury, MA.

transition period of 1708 to 1709 are the first to show up in the burying grounds of Byfield, Newbury, Rowley and Ipswich.

For the next ten years Hartshorn's work was well accepted in both Rowley and Ipswich where many of his stones still stand today. While living in Rowley he continued to make gravestones for Haverhill and Bradford until 1716, when Robert Mullicken, Sr. replaced him there. He also taught his new brother-in-law, Ezekiel Leighton of Rowley to carve gravestones. In 1719, his wife, Mary died and he remained there only a year or two more.[225] Afterwards, he moved again, this time to Norwich, Connecticut where he had other relatives. He lived into his eighties and continued to carve gravestones until he died in 1738.[226]

His work in Massachusetts has one consistent factor. He used lines to connect the mask like face and circles in the lunette. All his letters are upper case in the main epitaph. Some gravestones have extra wording on the bottom done in the lower case. The letter "U" is formed

---

[225] Tucker, 1992: 24 - 25.
[226] Benes, 1973: 161 - 162.

with slanting sides approximating a "V" and the "I" does not have a crossbar. The number 5 tips at a severe angle and the ampersand "&" is nearly horizontal on the line. The number 8 is formed by two circles. A few of his footstones have survived some of which have a top view of a coffin (See Fig. 24).[227]

---

[227] Tucker, 1989: 4.

Robert Mullicken, Sr. (1668 - 1741)

Carved:

Mother's Stone
Father's Stone
Milestone 36
Milestone 37 (1 of 4 carvers who worked on this stone)

In the late 1680's Robert Mullicken, Sr. came to Bradford where he settled at Kimball's Pasture. At the time, Bradford was still part of Rowley, a town established by weavers. In turn, it attracted other weavers like Robert because of its fulling mill. In 1687, Robert married Rebeckah Savory in Newbury. Over the years they had nine children.[228] He died June 11, 1741 and was buried in Bradford Burying Ground with a gravestone carved by his sons.

Bradford is located directly across the Merrimac River from Haverhill. In the early years, these towns were accessible to each other via a ferry. When Hartshorn began carving gravestones, people in both towns availed themselves of his services. This exposed Robert Mullicken to locally made gravestones.

Since both of these men were weavers it is likely they knew each other. This would account for Hartshorn's assistance in helping Robert when he began carving. Robert not only took up carving like Hartshorn, he did it later in life, in his mid-forties.[229]

In 1714, the first of Robert's gravestones began to show up in Bradford's burying ground and soon after, showed the influence of Hartshorn. By 1717, Mullicken completely replaced Hartshorn in Haverhill and Bradford.[230] His stones have the same mask like face and circle designs of Hartshorn's. However, from the start Mullicken distinguished himself from his predecessor by eliminating the curved lines in the lunette. Instead, he used non-connected

---

[228] Tucker, 1992: 25.
[229] Tucker, 1992: 25.
[230] Tucker, 1992: 24 -25.

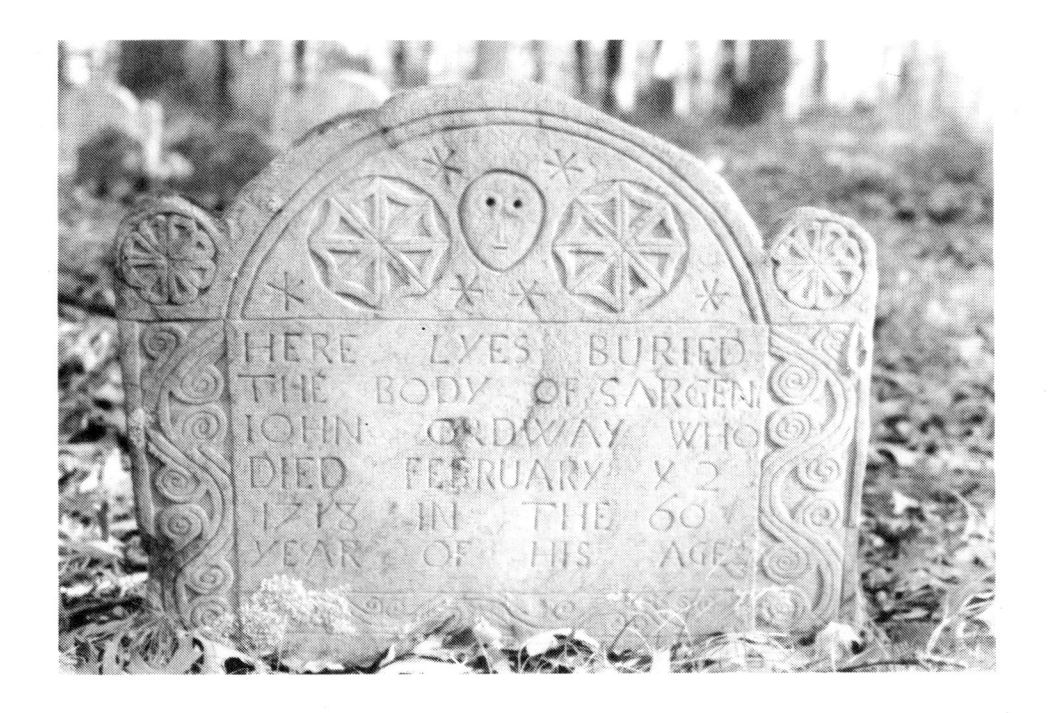

Fig. 27 – Sargent John Ordway's 1718 headstone with secondary designs of stars carved by Robert Mullicken, Sr. It is located in Sawyer's Hill Burying Ground, Newburyport, MA.

Fig. 28 – Mrs. Dorkes Bartlet's 1719 headstone shows Robert Mullicken, Sr.'s change from stars to mixed designs which include the stylized fleur-de-lis. It is located in Sawyer's Hill Burying Ground, Newburyport, MA.

designs to fill this space. These secondary designs changed every couple of years permitting a fairly accurate means to date his work.

The secondary designs, in 1718 began with stars and within two years were replaced with abstract designs (See Figs. 27 & 28). In conjunction with the abstract designs a stylized fleur-de-lis was used under the mask like face (See Fig. 28). Various forms of fleur-de-lis were used by Robert, Sr. throughout his career both as an armorial symbol and as a decorative design (see Fig. 29). One of these forms was a pair of plain fleur-de-lis along with a pair of hearts that he introduced in the year 1723 (See Figs. 58 & 60). These two designs were used only in the town of Newbury.

A year earlier, in 1722, Mullicken had picked up on the fact that symbolism could be used to show a person's social status. To denote Captain Attwood's importance, he carved three fleurs-de-lis on his footstone (Fig. 30) and a winged skull on his headstone. (Fig. 31) Atwood was one of two captains whose headstones deviated from the regular mask like face. Both have the winged skull, which set them above and apart from the regular people buried there. It was the design in widespread use by the professional carvers from Boston, whose gravestones were bought by the wealthy at the time. These are the only two gravestones with the skull and wings but not the only gravestones by Mullicken for Captains. The skull and wings design, a death symbol, was not well accepted locally, and it appears the Mullicken abandoned the use it after using it on these two Captain's headstones.

In 1723, Robert, Sr. incorporated symbolism on his gravestones for a very different reason, after he carved the Mother's and Father's stones. On these two portrait stones he had used symbolism to denote family heritage, love, and to show a relationship between two people. These ideas had evolved out of several sources, his own experiences with gravestone designs, Richard Dummer, Sr.'s use of fleur-de-lis on the 1636 and 1640 doorstones, and Hartshorn's work on milestone 33 and the 1690 doorstone. Hartshorn had used symbolism to link his two Dummer stones to the earlier 1636 doorstone through symbolic triangles.[231] Richard Dummer, Sr. had used the fleur-de-lis from his coat of arms to show his family heritage. Mullicken combined John Hartshorn's and Richard Dummer, Sr.'s use of symbolism with his own ideas. In

---

[231] See 1690 and 1708 stones for a detailed explanation.

Fleurs-de-lis of Robert Mullicken, Sr.

1715 (Set of two surrounding the face)
Armorial Design
Carved on one of Robert's earliest gravestones.

1719 (Single under the face)
Abstract Design

1720 (Single under the face)
Abstract Design

1722 (Single under the face)
Flower Design
Note how the tip emerges out of the top leaves.

1722 (Triple located on the footstone)
Armorial Design- Captain's gravestone.

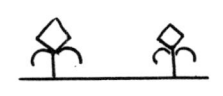

1723 (Double under the face)
Reproduction of 1636 doorstone

1723 (Double on the footstone)
Modified version of 1636 doorstone

1725 (Single under the face)
Flower Design

Fig. 29 – Fleur-de-lis designs used by Robert Mullicken, Sr.

turn, he went on and used two of the symbols (hearts and fleur-de-lis) on his gravestones in Newbury to denote the identity of the two people on the Mother's and Father's stones.[232]

This began with gravestones actually carved in 1723 and went on to those backdated for the same year. The backdating gave Robert an opportunity to match up dates, names and artwork on specific gravestones in order to leave the proper clues.[233] In those days, people gave the carvers their orders with the basic information (i.e., name, birth and death dates) and left the design to them. Carvers had the responsibility of choosing the artwork and wording.[234]

About 1725, Robert, Sr.'s production slows down and he begins to share the work with his sons, Robert, Jr. and John. They had previously apprenticed with their father to learn the gravestone carving trade. In 1727, the last year Robert, Sr. carved gravestones, he introduced a new design of multi-lined arches and a tall line with spirals under the mask like face (See Fig. 91). The multi-lined arch was later applied to his design on milestone 36.

In 1727, he turned the gravestone shop business over to his sons, but unbeknown to him his carving career was not yet finished. Six years later, Robert, Sr. took on his second major stone carving project. He and his three sons, who had become stone carvers, created and carved Newbury's boldy decorated milestones. Like the Mother's and Father's stones, the milestones challenged him in that the unique Dummer symbolism was once again incorporated. This project was the culmination of his stone carving career.

Robert's work is quite easy to recognize. He used the basic Merrimac Valley Style with a mask like face, and a circled design on either side in the lunette (See Fig. 32). For his secondary designs he used non-connected stars and abstract designs. Under the face, he favored a single stem with double spirals at the top or a stylized fleur-de-lis. All his letters are upper case except for a few lower case "t" and the word "the." On his "I" there is a crossbar that became a Mullicken family trademark. His eight's have a flat top. Many of his footstones are elaborately carved and use the same circled design as on the headstone. On his footstones there is a side view of a coffin.[235]

---

[232] See Mother's Stone and Father's Stone for a detailed explanation.
[233] See the Mother's Stone for a detailed explanation.
[234] Forbes, 1927: 15. On a rare occasion a customer would express a preference for one style of design over another (Stier, 1983: 72)
[235] Tucker, 1992: 27, 29, 32.

Fig. 30 – Capten Philip Atwood's 1722 footstone carved by Robert Mullicken, Sr. This is the first stone he introduced with a line of formal fleur-de-lis as a symbol of social rank. It is located in Bradford Burying Ground, Bradford, MA.

Fig. 31 – Capten Philip Atwood's 1722 headstone carved by Robert Mullicken Sr. The skull and wings design was copied from the professionally carved Boston gravestones. Mullicken used this non Merrimac Valley Style design to denote Atwood's social position.

Fig. 32 – Insin [Ensign] Benjamin Smith's 1723 headstone is an example of Robert Mullicken Sr.'s standard layout. It is located in Sawyer's Hill Burying Ground, Newburyport, MA.

Robert Mullicken, Jr. (1688 - 1756)

Carved:

Milestone 37 (1 of 4 carvers who worked on this stone)

Robert Mullicken, Jr. was one of three of Robert Mullicken, Sr.'s sons to follow him into the gravestone carving trade. He was the oldest child of Robert and Rebeckah Mullicken and was born in Bradford on December 8, 1688. Ralph Tucker feels Robert was married twice, first to Mary Hartbath which he could not confirm. In 1737 according to Bradford's vital records, Robert, Jr. married Mary Hoyt. Robert, Jr. was then forty-nine years old and Mary was about twenty-six. They went on to have a family of seven children all born in Bradford.[236] He died June 16, 1756 and was buried in the Bradford Burying Ground. His gravestone was carved by Joseph Marble and is still standing.

Before his father, Robert, Sr. died, he willed to Robert, Jr., his, "loom and tackling for weaving," six acres of land at "Dismal Hole" and other bequests.[237] Robert, Jr. like his father was a weaver and as an adult apprenticed with him to learn the gravestone carving trade.

Robert, Jr.'s artwork is traditional and competent but lacks creativity. Many of his secondary designs are poorly done because they were the work of apprentices. Throughout his life as a gravestone carver Robert, Jr. was forever the patient teacher. In the Mullicken gravestone shop his brother, Joseph apprenticed as well as several other unidentified carvers. The Websters and Marbles from Bradford both learned the trade there.[238] When Robert, Jr. carved gravestones by himself, as seen during the years 1735-36 it is evident he was a very capable and skilled carver. These two years appear to be the only ones he did not have an apprentice working with him.

His career begins in 1726 when he began to carve his own gravestones. His work is very similar to his father's later works with the standard raised design, four circled designs (two beside the face and one in each finial) and a mask like face. However, he developed his own

---

[236] Tucker, 1992: 32.
[237] Tucker, 1992: 32.
[238] Tucker, 1992: 25.

Fig. 33 – Mrs. Elisebeth Huse's 1735 headstone shows Robert Mullicken, Jr.'s use of molded arches between 1734 and 1736. His secondary designs differed from his father, Robert Mullicken, Sr. It is located in Sawyer's Hill Burying Ground, Newburyport, MA.

Fig. 34 – Mrs. Hannah Ayer's 1729 headstone shows the distinct poor quality workmanship of an apprentice working with Robert Mullicken, Jr. The apprentice carved the hearts and decorative lines under the face. It is located in the Pentucket Burying Ground, Haverhill, MA.

Stories Carved in Stone

Fig. 35 Abigail Allen's 1728 headstone shows that Robert Mullicken, Jr. favored the use of tall designs under the face. It is located in First Parish Burying Ground, Newbury, MA.

Fig. 36 – John Huse's 1736 footstone is an excellent example of Robert Mullicken, Jr.'s type of framing. He used a peaked box often topped with circles. It is located in Sawyer's Hill Burying Ground, Newburyport, MA.

identity through the use of different secondary designs (See Fig. 33). The letters he used were a mix of lower and upper case which further distinguishes his work from his father's.[239]

Robert along with his brother, John, took over the gravestone business in 1727. On a few probate records the two are both listed as being paid for the same gravestone, indicating a joint effort.[240] One of the several examples done by both Robert, Jr. and John is at Sawyers Hill on Susannah Morss's 1733 gravestone. The art work was carved by Robert, Jr. and the lettering was done by John. This was confirmed by two facts, John, who normally used all upper case "A's" made a rare exception and used a lower case "a" formed by a small loop and a large tail, the complete opposite of his brother, Robert's "a". Robert's lower case "a" has a large loop and small tail. The other fact is seen in the artwork by 1731 John had changed to a fan shaped whorl, whereas Robert, Jr. continued to carve a crescent shaped whorl. Susannah Morss's headstone not only has crescent shaped whorls but they are opposite facing, too. The whorls on her headstone are identical in style, except smaller, to the whorls on milestone 37.

While John and Robert, Jr. were operating the gravestone shop their brother, Joseph became an apprentice to them. In 1729, Robert's secondary designs show the distinct poor quality workmanship of an apprentice (See Fig. 34). Just as Robert had worked on his father's stones so did Joseph work on Robert, Jr.'s. Joseph also apprenticed with his brother, John, too. The Marble, Worster and Webster's families, also from Bradford, began carving at later dates.[241]

Robert, Jr. carved stones from 1726 to 1747.[242] He can be identified by several means. His secondary designs were carved with incised lines with the exception of three years. From 1734 to 1736, he used tall, molded arches (Fig. 33). Under the face, he favored tall designs often times separated into two parts (See Fig. 35). The letter "a" carved in both lower and upper case is frequently mixed on the same stone. His lower case "a" has a large bottom and small top. His work, like his father's, can be dated by the change in designs that occurred every couple of years.

On many of Robert's footstones he carved three plain circles on top of the framed house-like outline (See Fig. 36). He too, used a side view of a coffin and occasionally an hourglass with or without another design.

---

[239] Tucker, 1992: 33.
[240] Tucker, 1992: 32, 37.
[241] Tucker, 1989: 10-12.
[242] Tucker, 1992: 33.

John Mullicken (1690 - 1737)

Carved:

Milestone 35

Milestone 37 (1 of 4 carvers who worked on this stone)

John Mullicken was Robert, Jr.'s younger brother by two years. John was born on July 26, 1690 in Bradford. According to Ralph Tucker, John lived on an island in the Merrimac River between Bradford and Haverhill. His first marriage was to Mary Poore in 1717. They had four children. She died in 1728. Five years later, in 1733, John married his second wife, Sarah Griffin, and they had two children. He died "intestate" on November 4, 1737.[243] His main occupation was a blacksmith and secondary trade was as a gravestone carver.[244] His gravestone is next to his father's in the Bradford Burying Ground.

John had an artistic flare which was enhanced by new and creative methods he developed in carving. These gave a polished and sometimes sculptured look to his work. He incorporated these new techniques into the traditional Merrimac Valley Style on many of his gravestones. However, he periodically broke away trying different and creative designs. John was a perfectionist as seen in his artwork and from the fact he did not allow apprentices to work on his gravestones. Yet he was a good teacher as is witnessed by Joseph, who he influenced.

Tucker did an exhausted search of probate records and found the following items. In 1718, two payments were made to John from the estate of John Barnard of Salisbury. The account lists a pair of gravestones but not directly in association with the payments. The fact that one of the payments was for two pounds, the going price for a pair of stones, is suggestive that John was the carver of these gravestones. John is mentioned in 1722 and again in 1725 on another probate record, with his brother, "Robert and John Mulikin" however, neither of these two records mentions gravestones. One other probate record, Caleb Hopkinson 1732 lists the two brothers. Hopkinson's gravestone which is in Groveland burying ground was done by

---

[243] "Intestate" - Died without having written a legal Will. This is many times beneficial to historians because the courts or local officials would have to inventory the estate before dividing amongst the deceased's heirs.
[244] Tucker, 1992: 37.

Fig. 37 – Nicholas Colby's 1726 headstone is an early example of John Mullicken's work. It shows his experimentation with designs while maintaining the mask like face. This gravestone is located in First Parish Burying Ground, Newbury, MA.

Fig. 38 –Tristram Coffin's 1727 headstone reveals several changes that took place in John Mullicken's work in the early 1730's. It has the smoothly, rounded petals in the rosette, double lined and wide banded secondary designs in the corners, and the fan shaped whorl in the finial. It is located in First Parish Burying Ground, Newbury, MA.

Fig. 39 – Benaiah Titcom's 1728 headstone shows the flat raised method used by John Mullicken. It is located in First Parish Burying Ground, Newbury, MA.

Fig. 40 – John Stickney's 1733 headstone was John Mullicken's finest work. Carved about 1737, he achieved a sculptured look with the beautifully carved swirls. It is located in First Parish Burying Ground, Newbury, MA.

Robert, Jr.[245] These fragments are the only written records of John in the probate records. Previous research was unable to identify the gravestones carved by John possibly due to the fact his lettering was almost identical to his brother, Robert, Jr.'s. The only difference between the two brothers lettering is the letter "a" of which John used the upper case (A) the majority of the time with only a few exceptions.

The earliest surviving gravestones attributed to John show up about 1726. His designs are an assortment of ideas; some follow the traditional Merrimac Valley Style while others can only be recognized by the mask like face (See Fig. 37). The lettering varies from all upper case to a combination of upper and lower case. About 1729, he defines his style which is readily distinguished from his brother, Robert, Jr. John learned how to make a very smoothly rounded off design (See Fig. 38). It gives the appearance of having been sanded it is so smooth. Interlaced with this molded work are a few incised line designs on the same gravestones. While he was using this molded technique he worked on developing a wide-bladed whorl. By 1731/32 he changed his technique radically and began using a severe flat-raised method (See Fig. 39). Many of these type stones have a wide band completely surrounding the face and circles, as well as wide banded secondary designs. Between 1735 and 1736 he changed to a gravestone with a tall lunette and went to a very simplistic design style (See Fig. 86). During this period, several examples of his circled designs are simply circles inside circles. However, they are not simple. He attempted to carve them to give a sculptured look. On one, he mastered the sculptured look as exemplified by John Stickney's stone dated 1733 in First Parish that was lettered by his brother, Robert, Jr. (See Fig. 40). It is the only one of its kind by John.

John was adventuresome and experimented with both design layout and methods of carving. This led to the development of a fan-shaped whorl, that he used from 1731 onward for the rest of his career, a design, his brother, Robert, Jr. did not use. Like his father and brother, John's designs changed every couple of years which allows for fairly accurate dating.

From 1728 to 1737, John worked with his brother, Robert, Jr. and the two of them operated the gravestone shop. While working there, John took on his brother, Joseph as an apprentice. However, John took a different approach than Robert, Jr. He had Joseph do his own

---

[245] Tucker, 1992: 37-38.

gravestones with his assistance. This is evidenced by several gravestones which show John's distinctive style and designs but were obviously done by an apprentice.

The gravestones carved by John Mullicken can be identified in several ways. His secondary designs are usually raised and encircled by a wide-banded line. Under the face the design is low and spread out. In comparison his brother, Robert's are tall. In creating his designs he used three different methods. A well defined raised design with the background carved out, a smooth-rounded off type and a flared, fanned-out method (See Figs. 38, 39 & 40).

His lettering is the same as Robert, Jr.'s except for two letters. On the rare occasion he used the lower case "a" he carved it with a small bottom and large top. Some of his "L's" in the word "Lyes" slant forward noticeably.

The footstones that have survived vary considerably. He carved them with an incised line except for one in Newbury. Some have designs while others have only the name. A few were done without a coffin.

Joseph Mullicken (1704 - 1768)

Carved:

Milestone 37 (1 of 4 carvers who worked on this stone)

Joseph was Robert, Jr. and John's younger brother. He was born in Bradford on February 17, 1704. In 1736, he married Phebe Tylor at Bradford and during that same year joined his brothers in the gravestone business. Probate records indicate that Joseph had a number of occupations including, "yeoman, innholder, tavern keeper and ferryman."[246] He lived on Main Street in what is now Groveland, previously a part of Bradford. He died "intestate" in 1768 after becoming the most prolific stonecutter of the Mullicken family.[247] Joseph is buried in Riverview Cemetery, Groveland. His gravestone was carved by Joseph Marble, another gravestone carver from Bradford.[248]

Joseph was most likely a sociable person noted by the fact he was known as an innkeeper and tavern keeper. Like his brother John, he also had an artistic flare and was a perfectionist. Joseph was the most creative of the family breaking away from the traditional Merrimac Valley Style shortly after starting his career as a gravestone carver. This started with a wingless skull that evolved over the years into a pumpkin style face.[249] He seems to have had a freedom with his designs. His new designs were well accepted by the local people. Other gravestone carvers were also experiencing the same freedom with their designs during the years Joseph carved from the 1740's to 1760's.[250]

At age 15, in 1719, Joseph practiced carving his name on the bottom of a gravestone that his father had done (See Fig. 41). It is a backdated stone in Haverhill, dated 1718 with the deceased man's name of John (his last name has worn off). The letters show a glimpse of Joseph's artistic flare that was to come many years later.

When Joseph began to seriously apprentice in the Mullicken shop is uncertain. It may have been as early as 1729. In that year, the secondary designs on Robert, Jr.'s gravestones show

---

[246] Tucker, 1992: 39.
[247] Tucker, 1992: 39.
[248] Tucker, 1992: 25.
[249] Tucker, 1992: 46.

the work of an unskilled carver. A few years later, an apprentice, probably Joseph worked together with John, (only known example) on the same gravestone that of Mrs. Sara Brown dated 1732 (See Fig. 94). In Sawyers Hill Burying Ground, there are two gravestones believed to be some of Joseph's earliest stones. One is a traditional style made for Daniel Cheney, dated 1736, whose artwork and lettering were done under the guidance of Robert, Jr. The other was for Stephen Trustram, dated 1735 which shows the strong influence of his brother, John's style and designs. These examples, done by an apprentice almost ready to go out on his own are suggestive of Joseph, who has a documented gravestone payment in 1737.[251]

By 1737, Joseph began to carve gravestones on his own, using the traditional Merrimac Valley Style. Shortly thereafter, he introduced a radically new design, a wingless skull (See Fig. 42). These stones have a skull on a blank background that is flanked by two wide banded lines curled inward at the top. In the early 1740's the skull was modified and wings were added (See Fig. 43) The stark skull evolved first into a pear shaped face and about 1750 into a round pumpkin like face. After he introduced the pumpkin like face, Joseph stumbled upon the idea of a bonnet for women (See Fig. 44). From that point on he used a *bonnet* on the face of every woman's gravestone.[252] Here again is another example of men in colonial America publicly acknowledging women.

Joseph's designs were formed by using a sculptured like method developed by his brother, John. The influence John had on Joseph carried over to his side borders and finials until 1753, when he created his own *new* design. At that date, he changed over to a design in the side borders called a *bleeding heart* by gravestone researcher Ralph Tucker. In the finial he created a distinct flower formed by carving a small round button in the middle of a ring. The ring was molded to form a half round shape and carved with straight lines radiating out from the button to form the pedals (See Fig. 44). Noticeably absent are secondary designs in the lunette, after he introduced the skulls.[253]

---

[250] Deetz, 1977: 76, 79.
[251] Tucker, 1992: 39.
[252] Tucker, 1992: 39, 45, 46.
[253] Tucker, 1992: 46, 47.

Fig. 41 – The graffiti on this gravestone was done by Joseph Mullicken about age fifteen when he practiced carving his name. From the start he shows an artistic flare, the letter "J" is fancy, the "S" is double lined and the "H" on the line below has curled tops. (John ---- 1718 headstone, located in Pentucket Burying ground, Haverhill, MA.

Fig. 42 – Jonathan Colby's 1736 headstone is an excellent example of the skull Joseph Mullicken first used on his gravestones. It is located in the Church St. Cemetery, Merrimac, MA.

Fig. 43 – Mrs. Anna Roger's 1747 headstone has sculptured like wings added to the skull showing the influence John Mullicken had Joseph Mullicken's artwork. It is located in Sawyer's Hill Burying Ground, Newburyport, MA.

Fig. 44 – Mrs. Susanna Burbank's 1757 headstone with a bonnet on the pumpkin shaped head carved by Joseph Mullicken. It is located in Riverview Cemetery, Groveland, MA.

Joseph mastered lettering better than anyone else in his family. However, in his first year of carving, 1736, he started out using both upper and lower case letters like his brothers. The lettering, although the same as Robert, Jr.'s, is very poorly done therefore distinguishing it from his two brothers. This changed by 1738, when he went to all upper case with the exception of a lower case "t" which he used for the rest of his life. "In the early 1740s he adds a tail to the lower right of the letter "U," and he drops the letter "J" below the line when it begins a name."[254]

He carved gravestones up to 1766 just two years before he died at age 65. Of all the Merrimac Valley Style carvers, Joseph was the first to drift away from the original style creating in essence a style all his own. His style became popular with other local gravestone carvers who modified it to suite themselves.

---

[254] Tucker, 1992: 47.

The Newbury Carved Stones

The Carved Stones of the Dummer Farm

Introduction

From the perspective of the 20th century, the Newbury carved stones are a unique but obscure local anomaly. From the perspective of the 17th and 18th centuries, they would have fit comfortably into the artistic traditions of their times. They are unique only in the sense the decorative folk art designs were carved in stone rather than the more traditional materials like ceramics, canvas, silver, cloth and wood. Their historical importance comes not from their uniqueness, but rather from the fact they were a product of their times. They reflect the greater world around them. They give us some insight into the art of the 1600's and early 1700's, into the social traditions brought from the old world, and into how colonial men honored some of their women.

Five of the stones carved for the Dummer Family, graced their mansion house.[255] These stones were private art seen by family, relatives, and friends. In comparison, the milestones were works of art commissioned for public display. This is an important distinction, one which reflects changes in social attitudes and religious values which occurred between 1645 and 1735. The early laws of the Massachusetts Bay Colony banned conspicuous displays of wealth. Its meeting houses were plain and unornamented, and the exteriors of private residences were also plain. However, the control of the Puritan ministers and magistrates stopped at the front door of these private homes. Surviving pieces of ceramics, furniture, and other household goods attests to the fact art was very much present in their homes. Ceramics were decorated with abstract designs and painted with scenes from everyday life. Furniture contained carved details like geometric rosettes and other designs. Even the summer beams of the houses were nearly universally carved with a simple molded design called a chamfer. This artwork, however, has generally gone unnoticed because of the fact it is on everyday household items

---

[255] The 1636, 1640, 1690 doorstones and the Mother's and Father's Stones were found in the early 20th on the property of the old Alms House in Newbury, MA. Through extensive deed research, Lura Watkins (1969) determined that this was the site of the Dummer mansion house. The property is now the site of the Triton Regional School.

The Dummer carved doorstones standout because they are unique by our modern definitions of what constitutes art. However, in the mid 1600's when the first doorstones were carved, they would not have been a radical departure from the British cultural norms. The designs, the symbolism of the designs, and even the idea of carving the date on them were commonplace in England. What was different about them was that they were placed on a doorstone rather than a more prominent location on the house. Richard Dummer's mansion house being located five miles from the meeting house, gave him the opportunity to continue to practice the traditions his family enjoyed in England, but then officially banned in the Colony.

Grant it the artwork of the mid 1600's lacked the grace, elegance, and sophistication of the art found on furniture, ceramics, pewter, and silver pieces of the 1700's. However, it challenges our historical understanding of Puritan society as being plain and stoic. The Dummer carved stones mirror the changes in those art styles from the mid 1600's to the early 1700's. The first two doorstones designs are simple and conservative. In comparison, the Mother's and Father's stone reflect the greater elaboration and sophistication of the 1700's styles. And far from being new designs, the Mother's and Father's stones were reworked designs taken from gravestones and common everyday household ceramics.[256]

Placing designs on doorstones and walkway stones was an innovation that the Dummer's created. The idea of placing geometric designs, coats of arms, and other types of art on everyday utilitarian household items had been around for centuries. The 1636, 1640, 1690 doorstones and the Mother's and Father's stones are a product of their times. Their "uniqueness" gives us that rare chance to see for the first time, a fuller picture of the art which flourished in the early Colonial period.

---

[256] The authors came to these conclusions concerning the presence and transition of the arts in Puritan Society independently and unaware of previous research on this subject. However, the authors have since learned about and would recommend to those interested readers, the chapter on "John Hull of Boston, Goldsmith" in Samuel *Morison's Builders of the Bay Colony* (1981).

Fig. 45 – 1636 Doorstone
1636 Doorstone is in the collection of the Smithsonian Institution, National Museum of American History.
Used with permission.

1636 Doorstone

The 1636 doorstone has the earliest date, but was probably the second of the first two doorstones to be carved. (See Fig. 45) It was found on the Dummer's farm at "the Falls" where it had been carved between 1645 and 1679, for Richard Dummer, Sr. The doorstone has a date, two fleur-de-lis and a line of triangles. The date "1636" marks the year Dummer moved from Roxbury to Newbury verses the year he acquired the land. The artwork was derived from his coat of arms and English roof designs. In England, both armorial devices and geometric patterns were used to mark a person's estate and to decorate their houses. The carver was most likely a millwright.

The date "1636" was incised using a style common in the 1600's. The sixes indicate this fact, being formed by a circle with a tail added on top.[257] The number "3" in the date is proportionally smaller than rest of the numbers in the date. In comparison, the number "4" on the 1640 doorstone is proportionally larger than rest of the numbers in the date indicating that two stones were done by different carvers.

The two fleurs-de-lis are placed at each end, on opposite sides of the date. The design was carried over from the 1640 doorstone and placed in the upright position. On the 1636 doorstone, they were carved slanting outward unlike the 1640 doorstone where they are straight up and down. The fleur-de-lis comes from the Dummer coat-of-arms (See Fig. 4).

Under the date, space was allotted for a design. The design constitutes a line with three sets of triangles oriented downward. The middle triangle is repeated inside itself with single ones on either side of it. The triangle design appears to be purely decorative like similar designs on English roofs. (Fig. 46) Variations of these triangles went on to be used on the family's other stones, carved years later.

Between the sixteenth and seventeenth century, across southern England many houses were decorated on the outside. In the southeast, close to where Dummer came from, the roofs of houses were being covered with tile in elaborate patterns. Farther to the southwest in the

---
[257] Watkins, 1969: 6.

Cotswold area, roofs were finished off with decorated stone-slate verges[258]. Over in the east, in, "Norfolk, there were many thatched roofs, some with elaborate patterns created by the laying and cutting of reeds."[259] (See Fig. 47)

Armorial devices were another type of artwork used to decorate houses, an influence from sixteenth century feudal England.[260] Many manor houses and public buildings both inside and outside, had armorial devices like fleur-de-lis and coats of arms displayed. According to Barron Oswald, "A coat of arms is not held from the Crown, but is a piece of personal property, the right to which depends simply upon the user and the right as against others upon prior assumption."[261] This gives its owner the right to use it in whatever way he sees fit.

In New England a house built prior to 1755 at the corner of Garden Court Street and Bell Alley in Boston has the coat of arms of its original owner, William Clark. "The floors were of mahogany with the Clark coat of arms inlaid in the center of one of the parlors."[262] The coat of arms being inlaid in the floor corresponds to Dummer's doorstones in that each was walked on.

Richard, like others, brought his coat of arms, a part of his British heritage, with him when he settled in the Bay Colony. That same heritage placed a high value on land, which was passed on from one generation to the next. Richard, who was the first Dummer to emigrate, acquired a large tract of farm land. After which he encouraged other members of the Dummer family to emigrate and subsequently acquire farm land. The distinction of being the first Dummer in New England, may have contributed to him placing the fleur-de-lis from his coat of arms on both the 1636 and 1640 doorstones (See Fig. 48). Another reason for these doorstones could be because Dummer in the 1640's owned two other large farms. In Newbury near the main village, he owned three hundred acres and in Watertown he owned 500 acres. Placing dated and decorated doorstones at his mansion house distinguished it from his other properties.

It is not known who carved the 1636 doorstone. However, the workmanship attests to the fact that the person had extensive experience with stone carving. The lines are deep and have "V" shaped grooves. This strongly suggests the carver was a millwright. Richard Dummer employed a number of millwrights in the 1640's and 1650's to work on his mill and Nelson's mills.

---

[258] "Verge" - The edge of the tiling that projects over a roof gable. (Berube, 1985: 1343)
[259] Boumphrey, 1985: 13.
[260] Boumphrey, 1985: 11.
[261] Oswald, 1903: 162.
[262] Marlowe, 1954: 34.

Fig. 46 – Thatched roof with decorated patterns from cottage in Stow Longa, Huntingdon, UK.

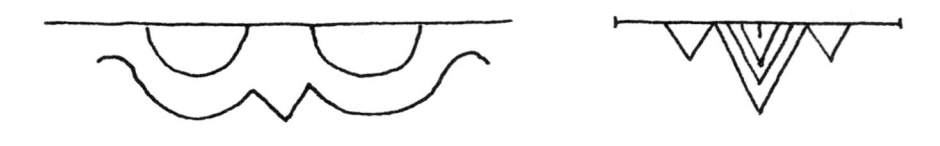

Fig. 47 – English cottage roof decorative pattern compared to 1636 Doorstone decorative design.

Fig. 48 – Formal fleur-de-lis compared to simple fleur-de-lis from 1636 & 1640 Doorstones.

The millwrights had extensive experience in shaping and sharpening the hard millstones. Given the doorstones were carved in hard diorite with deep lines, and the fact that Dummer employed a number of millwrights, it seems logical to conclude one them may have carved the doorstone.[263] Richard Dummer, Sr., himself, may have been the person who suggested the designs.

Dating the 1636 doorstone is problematic. The more elaborate design of the 1636 doorstone compared to the simple poorly composed design of the 1640 doorstone strongly suggests it was the second doorstone to be completed. The 1640 doorstone is dated to circa 1640-1645. The 1636 doorstone therefore was done after 1645 and prior to 1679 when Richard Dummer Sr. died. There is insufficient evidence to narrow the date down any further.

Dummer was arguably slightly head of his times in the use exterior house decorations in the Massachusetts Bay Colony. According to architectural historian Abbott Lowell Cummings, "little bursts of decorative exuberance are confined almost entirely to the last quarter of the seventeenth century."[264] In this statement, Cummings is referring to interior and exterior house embellishments of chamfered beams, molded first story post heads, second floor extended beams supporting overhangs, and dropped pendants at corners of second story overheads.

Richard Dummer, Sr.'s doorstones were the forerunner of a new emerging social trend in interior and exterior architectural decorations that emerged after 1670. There are a number of surviving examples of these decorations. The John Knowlton House in Ipswich, MA has a fireplace lintel with "a horizontal creased molding, a beaded lower edge, and the same kind of compass decoration with punch marks that one finds on seventeenth-century chests and boxes." The punch marks are in the shape of a diamond. The lintel is dated to 1670-1689.[265] The Hart House from Ipswich MA has a fireplace lintel with alternating raised squares in a row.[266] A 17th century architectural over-hang pendant (attributed to Newbury, MA) has four hearts cut out.[267] The Old Feather Store in Boston MA (demolished in 1860) had extensive exterior decoration on its plastered walls. This decoration included the date "1680", hearts, repeated patterns of squares, and diamonds.[268]

---

[263] See pp. 21-22 for the names of the millwrights employed by Dummer.
[264] Cummings, 1979: 127.
[265] Cummings, 1979: 179.
[266] Cummings, 1979: 180 (see caption).
[267] Cummings, 1979: 179.
[268] Cummings, 1979: 37 (photo), 135, 136.

Fig. 49 – 1640 Doorstone.
1640 Doorstone is in the collection of the Smithsonian Institution, National Museum of American History.
Used with permission.

1640 Doorstone

No historical records exists that mention the 1640 doorstone (Fig. 49), who carved it, or when it was carved. However, the historical events of 1640, the events in Richard Dummer Sr.'s life, and evidence from the 1640 doorstone itself offer some clues to these questions. All of the combined evidence suggests that the 1640 doorstone was carved by a local millwright between the years 1640-1645, and that stone marked the year Dummer built his house on the farm at "The Falls" in Newbury.

The date 1640 offers some explanation. In May of 1640, the law prohibiting citizens from building beyond a half mile distance from the Meeting House was repealed. Richard Dummer, Sr. whose farm was five miles distance from the meeting house had been affected by this law. The repeal of the law must have been a welcomed event for Dummer. The fact that Dummer chose the 1640 date for the doorstone is strong evidence that he began construction of his house on his farm property near "The Falls" in that year.

The 1640 doorstone was deeply incised with only a date and a pair of fleur-de-lis. The date, 1640, has a 1600's style six that was formed by a circle with a tail. Its tail was carved to flow into the circle with a fluid motion unlike the tail on the 1636 doorstone which is clearly attached. The depth and sureness of all the incised lines, along with the workmanship on the six shows the work of a skilled stone cutter. The upside down fleur-de-lis placed on each end of the date, look too big because the flower head drops below the date. This throws the whole design out of balance indicating the stone cutter did not have any artistic training.

The confident stone carving work but poor artistic skills suggests that it was carved by a millwright. Millwrights were skilled in shaping and sharpening millstones from hard stones. This would account for the carver's ability to cut deep incised lines into the extremely hard diorite doorstone. Both Dummer and Thomas Nelson of Rowley added grist mills to their existing sawmills in the early 1640's. Dummer built his mill sometime between 1638 and 1645,[269] and Nelson built his between 1644 and 1645.[270] Richard Holmes, a millwright, was hired to build the Nelson's gristmill. Holmes states, "... I wrought at above said Mills, at Mr Nellsons Charge, to

---

[269] Currier, 1902: 38-39, 156, 649; Watkins, 1969: 9.
[270] Gage, 1840: 410.

build said Mills & Dams & make ye stones for said Grist Mill...."[271] Mark Prime was hired to operate the mill.[272] There is no record of who Dummer hired to build and operate his own grist mill at "The Falls." However, it is possible it was the same two workmen that Nelson had employed.

Dummer had firmly established his family at the Newbury farm at the Falls by 1645. He remarried in 1643 and brought his wife and her children from a previous marriage to the farm. In 1645, his son Jeremiah was born at the farm. His grist mill was also in full operation by 1645. This strongly suggests that a doorstone marking the beginning of his permanent residence on the farm in 1640, would have not have been carved any later than 1645.

---

[271] Jewett and Jewett, 1946: 170-171.
[272] Essex County MA, 1912: (vol. 2) 20-21.

Stories Carved in Stone

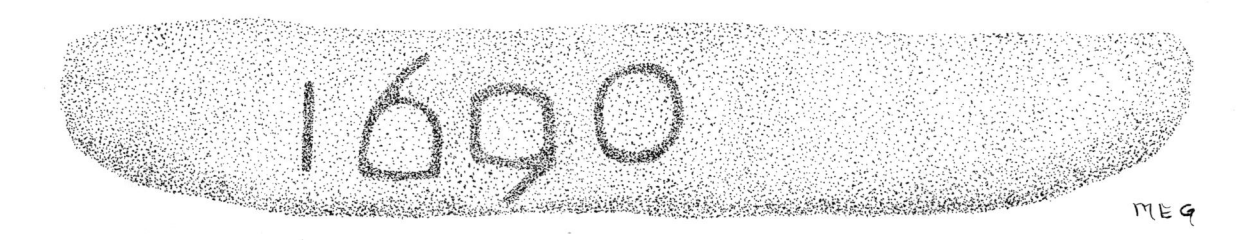

Fig. 50 – 1690 Doorstone (Front Edge)
1690 Doorstone is in the collection of the Smithsonian Institution, National Museum of American History.
Used with permission.

Fig. 51 – 1690 Doorstone (Top Surface)
1690 Doorstone is in the collection of the Smithsonian Institution, National Museum of American History.
Used with permission.

1690 Doorstone

The odd date "1690" on this doorstone has no significance except that it indicates the year it was carved in. It was chiseled into the stone in a very crude manner by someone with no stone carving experience (See Fig 50). In direct comparison, the geometric designs on top show the workmanship of a skilled stone carver (See Fig. 50).

1690 was just one year after young John Dummer was willed his father, Richard, Jr.'s estate. This inheritance included the two early doorstones that greatly impressed him, making John, the logical person to have carved the date, trying to imitate his grandfather. Everything points to John doing it while he was a young teenager. The numbers are crude and poorly carved using straight lines that form box shaped numerals. Furthermore, the date is off center. Twenty years later, when John had the services of an actual stone carver, John Hartshorn, he had designs placed on the top surface. This indicates that the doorstone with its poorly carved date meant a great deal to him, for he had the wealth to have a whole new doorstone made.

The crudely carved date cannot be mistaken for John Hartshorn's work. He was an accomplished stone carver by then, who would not have made such a grievous error in placing the date off center. Hartshorn's previous work on the 1708 milestone shows he had mastered his craft[273]. Not only is the date centered on the milestone, but so is the double triangle, which was placed directly under it.

The top surface of the 1690 doorstone was carved with geometric designs by John Hartshorn circa 1709 (See Fig. 51). This was a new concept, for the first two doorstones were carved only on their front edges. On this doorstone the designs were placed on the surface that was walked on. However, this top surface was rough with a damaged corner which Hartshorn left blank. This was rather unusual for the time and may be due to his lack of exposure to other carvers work. Master craftsmen (gravestone carvers) carved damaged corners right along with the rest of the stone as though nothing was amiss with the stone.

To create the geometric design Hartshorn used two or more sources; the artwork on the 1636 doorstone, Richard Dummer, Jr.'s gravestone and/or his own design. The design layout consists of circles in the corners and triangles placed on the edge in between. The circle design is a set of two circles, one inside the other with a dot in the middle. In the finial on Richard Dummer, Jr.'s gravestone there is a plain circle with a small inner circle and dot (See Fig. 7). However, when Hartshorn carved John & John Rolfe's gravestone (circa 1706-1708), he used the same circle design (See Fig. 52). This earlier circle design was possibly borrowed from professionally carved Boston gravestones. It is unknown whether the circles were meant to be a family link or decorative designs.

Fig. 52 – John & John Rolfe's double headstone with Hartshorn's use of repeated circles inside themselves. It is located in Pentucket Burying Ground, Haverhill, MA.

Another aspect, he seems to have picked up from the professionals, was the idea of placing designs on the top surface and in each corner. Colonel Pierce's 1701 slab top tombstone in First Parish, which lays flat on the ground and faces upwards has the same basic layout, with a design in its top two corners. An example of Hartshorn knowing and using this set up is seen on Mary Sawyer's 1708 footstone (See Fig. 53). The triangles originated from the design on the 1636 doorstone. This design has exactly the same number of triangles, three, repeated inside

---

[273] See the 1708 Milestone for a detailed explanation.

each other, as the middle set on the 1636 doorstone. However, he eliminated the bottom line on the triangles leaving it open ended. Being placed on the very edge as it was may have contributed to this factor. This set of triangles makes a strong connection to the 1636 doorstone, which in turn forms a Dummer family link between the two doorstones.

In the year 1709, Hartshorn experimented with various ways of using circles, which aided in dating this doorstone. The stylistic components used on the doorstone were afterwards integrated into his designs on gravestones. On one gravestone, he cut the circle in half and repeated it around the inside edge of a large circle (See Fig. 54). This shows striking similarity to the open-ended triangles on the doorstone. Another gravestone has a circle with small whole circles around the inside edge, showing a repeated design pattern (See Fig. 55). Both of these gravestones are dated 1709 with circled designs in the lunette, a style he had only started to use a year earlier. A list in Puritan Gravestone Art of all his gravestones reveals his heaviest use of *circle*s was between 1708 and 1709.[274] They show up in the side border design of the ornate bell, within circles in the lunette and finials, even as the top of a crown. The following year, 1710, his side border and circled designs change. By then, his designs were being influenced by new ideas he was seeing on the imported Boston gravestones. This evidence strong suggests that the top surface of the 1690 Doorstone was carved circa 1709.

Fig. 53 (Left) – Mary Sawyer's 1708 footstone patterned after Colonel Pierce's tombstone.
Sawyer Hill Burying Ground, Newburyport, MA / First Parish Burying Ground, Newbury, MA.
Fig. 54 (Center) – Circle design in lunette of Henery Lunt's 1709 gravestone.
First Parish Burying Ground, Newbury, MA.
Fig. 55 (Right) – Finial design on Samuel Gill's 1709 headstone.
First Burying ground, Salisbury, MA.

---

[274] Slater, Tucker, Farber: 1978.

Fig. 56 – Mother's stone
The Mother's stone is in the collection of the Smithsonian Institution, National Museum of American History.
Used with permission.

Mother's Stone

My ever <u>honoured</u> and most dear mother was translated to heaven.[275]

Simon Bradstreet
September 16, 1672

The Mother's stone is a doorstone with the head of a woman surrounded by hearts, flowers and the sun (See Fig. 56). Carved in 1723, it was a memorial to Elizabeth Dummer, John Dummer's mother. For this doorstone, John Dummer went to another carver because Hartshorn had moved to Connecticut. He was Robert Mullicken, Sr. from Bradford, who had become an accomplished rural gravestone carver by this time. The doorstone reflects Robert Mullicken, Sr.'s gravestone carving style in particular his use of non-connected designs. Mullicken also emulated John Hartshorn's example of linking the various Dummer carved stones together through borrowing symbolic designs from previous stones (in this case a link to the 1636 and 1690 doorstones). The carving on this doorstone is simplistic and contains some mistakes. However, Mullicken did master the expression of ideas in the form of art. In the design he embodies mother, matriarch, family heritage and symbolism.

The Mother's stone and its counterpart the Father's stone are different from all the other Dummer stones in that they are portrait type stones. For these two stones John Dummer may have had some input on what kind of design was used. In the Risley Papers from a family gravestone shop in Vermont, there are several examples of personal requests in regards to what the customer wanted (i.e. design, size of stone, and wording.) In 1784, the order written by Rev. John Smith Professor of Learned Languages at Dartmouth College for his wife's gravestone made two requests, "You will ingrave this in the order as it stands, without a deaths head." Rev. Smith had sent an order with instructions as to what wording he wanted on the gravestone and asked for an alternative design to the death head.[276] This is in contrast to an order sent into the Mullicken shop in 1736 where by the customer simply gave the carvers the pertinent information. That order reads, "Mr. Robert Mulican of Bradford Ser pray make; for me Two Gravestones; One

---

[275] Morison, 1981: 335. Emphasis added.

for David Foster jeunier...........and when they are made; send me word; and I will come and pay you for them."[277] Gravestone carvers for the most part had creative freedom in their work yet they also had to please their customers.

To trace the origins of the Mother's stone two questions need to be addressed. What do the symbols represent and how do they relate to the Dummers? Also, to understand the Mother's stone, it is necessary to discuss the Father's stone, which was carved in the same year. These two stones are connected by the same symbol: a circle with a dot in the middle which was reserved for and used only on these two stones. The idea of showing a relationship between two individual people through the use of a specific symbol was a concept Mullicken developed.

A year before, in 1722, Mullicken had started to use symbolism on his gravestones, to acknowledge people he felt were important. This occurred on two captains' gravestones on which he used a skull with wings in the lunette (See Fig. 31). On Captain Phillip Atwood's footstone stone he carried the idea further by carving three fleur-de-lis (See Fig. 30). The fleur-de-lis symbol was then being used by professional gravestone carvers to show a person's high social status but was restricted to Colonels or men with the title Very Honorable. Hartshorn, who had influenced Mullicken, in 1708, had previously picked up on the fleur-de-lis use as a status symbol and applied it to a woman's gravestone in Newbury. He did this to denote the fact she was the first member of the Sawyer family to be buried in Sawyers Hill Burying Ground. Hartshorn, who lacked formal training, had become aware that the professionals were setting woman apart with elaborately carved gravestones and did likewise with a local woman whom he felt was important. Mullicken, who studied the artwork on other gravestones, as seen in his own designs, had unlimited access to both the professional carvers and Hartshorn's work that appeared in Newbury, Ipswich, Rowley, and other towns.

Mullicken combined his knowledge of designs that made a person stand out with two symbols from the Mother's stone and carved them on gravestones in Newbury dated 1723. These designs secretly left clues to the identities of the people portrayed on the Mother's and Father's stones. This was done by use of symbols (designs) on selected gravestones which showed the various relationships between mother and son, wife and husband, a man named John, the town of Newbury and the year 1723. This appears to be an afterthought, as it started on a

---

[276] Stier,1983: 72.

stone dated 1724, on the part of Mullicken but it is extremely useful in tracing the meaning behind the symbols on the Mother's and Father's stones. The symbols were pairs of fleur-de-lis and pairs of hearts. The fleur-de-lis denotes *military officers,* persons of *high social status*, and in the case of the Dummers a symbol from their coat-of-arms. The hearts were used on gravestones with the *first name of John* and indicate someone by that name was involved with the two portrait stones. Furthermore, both symbols were used on Mullicken carved gravestones to show relationships between individuals: *Husband / Wife* and *Mother / Son*. This occurred only in the town of Newbury and only on gravestones dated 1723 with one exception in 1724.

The first symbolic clues are found on Abigail and Samuel Sawyer's headstones. On their headstones, Mullicken followed his usual pattern and made each one different with the exception of a single symbol. This was the fleur-de-lis symbol, although a single on one and a pair on the other, it makes a connection between husband and wife. Abigail's headstone has Mullicken's regular stylized fleur-de-lis which was carved first (1722) (See Fig. 57). Samuel's headstone has a pair like those on the Mother's stone and was the second to be done (1723) (See Fig. 58).[278]

Pairs of fleur-de-lis were also used for the purpose of denoting a soldier. A double pair of fleur-de-lis was given to Ensign Joseph Knight (See Fig. 59), who had the symbol placed on both his headstone and footstone. Another soldier who died in 1723, Ensign Benjiamin Smith, has a pair on his footstone. The gravestones of soldiers who died from 1724 onward in time do not have fleur-de-lis and of soldiers who died before this year, only one has the symbol. It was used to denote a captain who was given three fleurs-de-lis.

The symbolic pair of fleur-de-lis appears on one other footstone, that of John Sawyer which is a backdated stone. John was Mary Sawyer's son on whose footstone Hartshorn many years earlier had carved the fleur-de-lis symbol to show her social status. The other symbol, a pair of hearts, appears on John Sawyer's headstone (See Fig. 60). It connects him to his mother, Mary, who had hearts on her headstone. John's pair of hearts is in the lunette, while his mother has them intricately carved into the side border designs. (See Fig. 25) The hearts do more than

---

[277] Quoted in Forbes, 1927: 15.
[278] Some of the work on Samuel Sawyer's headstone was done by an apprentice working in Robert Mullicken, Sr.'s shop

Fig. 57 – Abigail Sawyer's 1722 headstone with a stylized fleur-de-lis carved by Robert Mullicken, Sr. It is located in Sawyer's Hill Burying ground, Newburyport, MA.

Fig. 58 – Samuel Sawyer's 1723 headstone with pair of fleur-de-lis carved by Robert Mullicken, Sr. It is located in Sawyer's Hill Burying ground, Newburyport, MA.

Stories Carved in Stone

Fig. 59 – Ensign Joseph Knight's 1723 footstone with a pair of fleur-de-lis carved by Robert Mullicken, Sr. It is located in First Parish Burying Ground, Newbury, MA.

Fig. 60 – John Sawyer's 1723 headstone with a pair of hearts carved by Robert Mullicken, Sr. It is located in Sawyer's Hill Burying ground, Newburyport, MA.

link him to his mother they represent a man named *"John" and "son"*. He is one of the three men, whose first name is *John*, who died between 1723 and 1724, who Mullicken carved gravestones for. All three have a pair of hearts in the lunette.

The other two people from Newbury with hearts are John Knight (1723) in Sawyers Hill and John Brown (1724) in First Parish. John Brown's 1724 headstone gives some clue to the fact Mullicken picked up on some of his ideas as time went on. These three people are the only ones on whom Robert Mullicken, Sr. used the heart symbol in this manner. Hearts by Robert Mullicken, Sr. are found on only one occasion after that, they were used on the footstone of Isaac Bayliy [Bailey] in 1726. Here he broke away from the headstone and placed the hearts on a footstone, in this case to denote an important member of the local parish and head of his household. These are the only known examples of hearts used by Robert Mullicken, Sr. and should not be confused with other examples used by his sons.

The various relationships and use of symbols correspond to Dummer family members involved with the two stones carved with human images. They are Captain Richard Dummer, military officer, husband and father, who is depicted on the Father's stone. Elizabeth Dummer, Richard's wife and mother of John, who is depicted on the Mother's stone. John Dummer, their son, who ordered these stones.

The following is a breakdown of how the symbols were specifically used on gravestones to relate to the Dummers. Captain Richard Dummer, the *military officer*, is represented by the two soldier's graves. Richard and Elizabeth, who are *husband and wife*, are denoted by Samuel and Abigail Sawyer's graves. Elizabeth and John, who are *mother and son*, are depicted through the graves of Mary and her son John Sawyer. John Dummer, who ordered the stones, is denoted by gravestones with the combination of hearts and the first name "*John.*" The social status of the Dummers is played out through the Sawyers with fleur-de-lis on their gravestones. The Sawyers with this symbol, Mary, John, Samuel and Abigail have the status of being buried in a public burying ground named after their family.[279]

This ingenious use of symbolism by Robert Mullicken, Sr. gives some insight into what the rural craftsmen were capable of doing.

---

[279] See Appendix B for a complete list of all the gravestones and relationships.

Origins of the Designs on the Mother's Stone

When Robert Mullicken, Sr. created the Mother's stone he drew on various sources for ideas. The ideas came from gravestones carved by both, the Boston carvers and John Hartshorn, the Dummer doorstones, English ceramic wares, and silversmith, Jeremiah Dummer's maker's mark. For the layout he relied on his method of non-connected secondary designs. Interestingly, this layout was in style and being used on ceramic wares from England during this period.[280]

The Mother's stone consists of a framed portrait surrounded by hearts, fleur-de-lis, circles and a sun. The top edge of the approximately 3' x 3' stone is scalloped and the 15" width (side view) is incised with crosshatching with a dot in the squares. It is an impressive stone carved with eighteenth century folk art.

The woman's face was designed after the cherub like face with human features on a Boston carved gravestone dated 1717, for Major Daniel Davison, in First Parish Burying Ground, Newbury (See Fig. 61). On the Mother's stone, the face is a bit crude but shows a great effort to make it human like. She has well defined oval eyes and a nose that widens at the bottom to resemble the same human feature, although it was created with straight lines. The lips are mere dots with a solid down curved line placed beneath them to create a chin. Another feature is the hair which Mullicken duplicated from the cherub on Davison's gravestone. Both the portrait and the cherub have hair that parts in the middle on top of the head with rounded curls down the either side of their faces and long curls turned outward beside the chin.

Under the face is a triangular design. On Mullicken's gravestones an abstract design was carved under every face. It is undetermined what this particular triangle represents. The triangle does not have a flat top instead the lines are slanted slightly down toward the middle point. However, it is of triangular shape, indicating a possible link to the triangles on the other Dummer stones.

The portrait is enclosed by a frame and is placed in the middle of the stone. The same concept is seen on a salt-glazed stoneware tankard from England, dated circa 1700 - 1725.[281] It has a free standing portrait enclosed in a frame (See Fig. 62).

---

[280] Stillinger, 1972: 91.
[281] Stillinger, 1972: 91. Note: The Nelson-Atkins Museum of Art cataloging information lists the date of this piece as 1740. The date provided by Stillinger (circa 1700-1725) is more in line with the folk art motifs on the piece.

Fig. 61 – Major Daniel Davison's 1717 headstone done by a professional Boston carver. Robert Mullicken Sr. modeled the face on the Mother's stone after the cherub on this headstone. It is located the First Parish Burying Ground, Newbury, MA.

Fig. 62 – Circa 1700-1725 English ceramic tankard with framed face portrait and full length man posed with outward turned feet along with hand on hip. The framed face portrait of the Mother's stone and full length man's pose of the Father's stone were common folk art motifs during the early 1700's. (Drawing based upon photographs.)
The Nelson-Atkins Museum of Art, Kansas City, Missouri (Purchase: Nelson Trust) 54-12.
Used with permission.

Mullicken has one example, showing he experimented with a free standing frame on John Brown's headstone, dated 1724, in the First Parish Burying Ground. By 1723, when Mullicken carved the Mother's stone, he was using a frame with three arches that formed curves over the two circled designs and head in the lunette. The doorstone's frame with its odd shape appears to be a compilation of both the tankard and gravestone frames (See Fig. 63). The top half resembles the tankard (See Fig. 64), but the bottom half looks like the top of the frame used in his lunette (See Fig. 65). This gave the frame, two arched curves under the face that he filled with a circle with a dot in the middle. These curves underneath the face and neck piece make the circles inside them, look like breasts. This is a misconception. They are simply another version of the circled design used by Hartshorn.

The circle with the dot is a modified version of John Hartshorn's double circle with a dot found on the 1690 doorstone. Mullicken modified Hartshorn's design as a means of distinguishing himself from his predecessor. Secondly, he created a symbolic link to the 1690 doorstone in the same way that Hartshorn did when he modified the triangle design on the 1708 milestone to link it to the 1636 doorstone.

The hearts were both a symbol of love and another piece of family iconography. The makers mark of Jeremiah Dummer, the silversmith, who was John's uncle, has a heart with his initials and a fleur-de-lis inside (See Fig. 66).[282] An example of hearts used by Robert Mullicken, Sr. is found on John Sawyer's (1723) headstone (See Fig. 60).

The fleur-de-lis was derived from the 1636 doorstone. A pair that matches these is found on the headstone of Samuel Sawyer (1723) in Sawyers Hill Burying Ground (See Fig. 57). Another example of a pair is on Ensign Joseph Knight's (1723) footstone in First Parish Burying Ground (See Fig. 59). Only Robert Mullicken, Sr. used pairs of fleur-de-lis, his sons used other versions such as single and triple with one exception. Robert Jr. used a pair of fleurs-de-lis once in his career (Mary Griffing 1728, Bradford Burying Ground, Bradford, MA).

The sun appears to be an afterthought. It is a circle with a dot in the middle with lines radiating out to form the sun. An example of a design placed directly over the face is seen on Lt. Samuel Sawyer's 1718 headstone (See Fig. 67). On this gravestone a star was used.

---

[282] Clarke, Foote: 1935; Bigelow, 1917: 18.

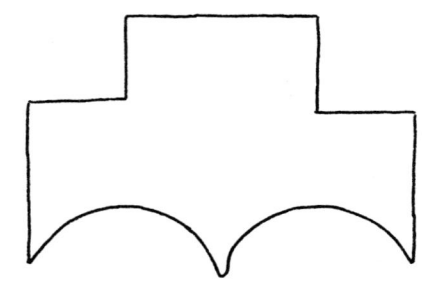

Fig. 63 – The frame on the Mother's stone. It is a compilation of the frame style on the tankard and the frame Robert Mullicken Sr. used on his gravestones from 1720 onwards.

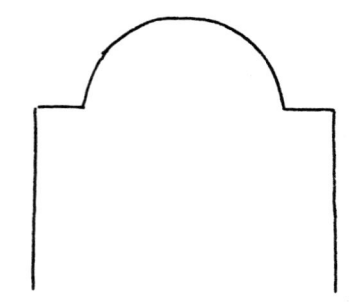

Fig. 64 – Top portion of the frame surrounding the face shown on the tankard in Fig. 62.

Fig. 65 – The three half circles that were used as a frame in the lunette on Roberk Mullicken Sr.'s gravestone from 1720 onward.

Fig. 66 – Maker's mark of Jeremiah Dummer, silversmith.

Fig. 67 – Lt. Samuel Sawyer's 1718 headstone shows how Robert Mullicken Sr. used a star directly over the head like the sun on the Mother's stone. It is located in Sawyer's Hill burying Ground, Newburyport, MA.

Fig. 68 – John Brown's 1724 headstone with a scalloped frame and a pair of hearts carved by Robert Mullicken Sr. It is located in First Parish Burying Ground, Newbury, MA.

The scalloped edge around the semi-circular stone gives a beautiful finished look to it. The only example of a scallop edged frame on a gravestone is found on John Brown's 1724 headstone in the First Parish Burying Ground, Newbury, MA (See Fig. 68.) The crosshatching on the 15" thick side (See Fig. 11) was used on gravestones but without the dots. It was placed under the body of letters on a number of headstones from 1716 to 1718 and again in 1723.

An overview study of Mullicken's gravestones shows he changed his secondary designs every year or two. The stars used in 1718 transition to a combination of stars and fleur-de-lis in 1719. In 1720 the stars are dropped and replaced with abstract designs, often in conjunction with a fleur-de-lis. By following these design changes, his gravestones and his other carved stones can be dated.

The fleur-de-lis gave the most precise date for the Mother's stone. Mullicken used this symbol from the beginning of his carving career. He used it as both an armorial and decorative design. By 1722, he had perfected a stylized fleur-de-lis that resembled a flower which he kept for the duration of his career with one exception. In the year 1723, he used pairs of simple, plain fleur-de-lis. These pairs only show up that year and only in the town of Newbury. In addition, Mullicken only carved pairs of hearts on headstones during the years 1723/24 and only in the town of Newbury. This evidence indicates that the Mother's stone was carved in 1723.

This doorstone was most likely used in conjunction with the Father's stone.[283] Its straight edge would have been placed up against the house with the rounded edge facing outward. The placement presented a view from two angles. When people walked up to the house, they saw the scalloped and crosshatched edge. When they left the house, the face surrounded with designs representative of Elizabeth Dummer looked up at them. It was a very practical way to present the doorstone, in which its top surface could be fully viewed and appreciated.

---

[283] See the Father's Stone for a detailed explanation.

Father's Stone

The Father's stone is a full length carving of a 1600's gentleman. It is a memorial to Captain Richard Dummer (1649-1689), commissioned by his son John Dummer, and carved by Robert Mullicken, Sr. in circa 1723 (See Fig. 69). This was the second of a pair, the first being the Mother's stone, a memorial to Elizabeth Dummer, John's mother. It is 4 feet 4 inches tall, 1 foot 8 inches wide at the bottom, and 2 feet 4 inches wide at the top.

The Father's stone, which is a little different, was probably used in the walkway leading to the house. Several variations in its carving and shape make this apparent when compared with the doorstones. At the top of the stone it is thick on the right side (13 inches) and thin (3 inches) on the left side making it unstable as a doorstone. The sides do not have any designs, allowing it to be sunk flush with the surface of the ground as a means to stabilize it. In comparison, the other doorstones with dates and designs on their narrow sides needed to be placed on top of the ground to be viewed. Finally, its figure was carved down the full length of the stone suggesting it was placed lengthwise. The only practical way to use this stone was in a walkway. Given that the man and woman represented by the Mother's and Father's stone were husband and wife suggests that these two stones may have been arranged together at one of the entrances to the mansion house. Figure 70 illustrates one possible arrangement of these two stones together.

The Father's stone was carved with the full figure of a gentleman surrounded with circles and a triangle at the bottom. This unusual carving is very similar to designs on ceramic wares being imported from England between 1700 and 1725. Although kitchen, dairy and other traditional utilitarian wares were being made in the colony at the time, decorative ceramic wares were still being imported. "Every one Incourages the Growth and manufactures of this Country and not one person but discourages the Trade from home, and says 'tis pitty any goods should be brought from England,' said one Bostonian in 1718."[284]

Robert Mullicken, Sr., who had no training in art, relied heavily on finding designs for his carved stones, from artwork done by other people. In 1714, when he started needing designs

---

[284] Stillinger, 1972: 89.

Fig. 69 – The Father's stone.
The Father's stone is privately owned by the Woodbury Family.
Used with permission.

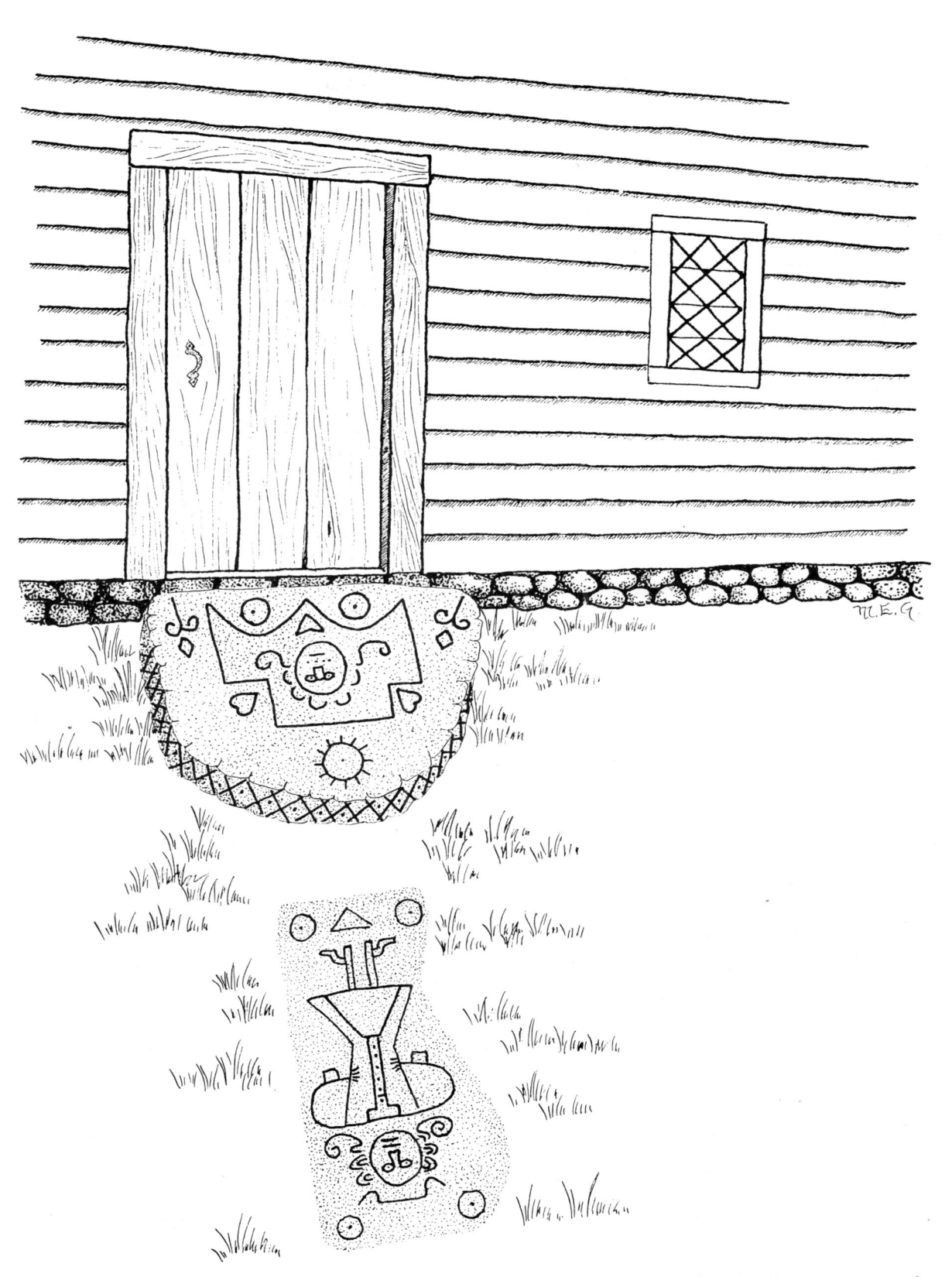

Fig. 70 – The Mother's and Father's stones may have been arranged at the Dummer mansion house as shown in the above artist's rendition.

for his gravestones, he had Hartshorn's and other professional's artwork on gravestones as sources. For the Father's and Mother's stones he expanded these sources to include the designs on ceramic wares from England. In the seventeenth century, Thomas Toft from Staffordshire created Toft wares with decorative art and became, "noted for his lively and original pottery."[285] An example of his work on a plate shows a gentleman in a tight-fitting, flared skirt coat with his arms raised above his head holding an object (?). He is facing forward with his legs spread apart and his feet turned out in opposite directions. The background space is filled in with non-connected abstract and geometric flower like designs. The plate's edge is finished off with a crosshatching pattern.[286]

This decorative art evolved and was used by other artisans to create designs on many different ceramic wares. Between 1700 and 1725, a more refined version of the above gentleman was depicted on a brown salt-glazed stoneware tankard from England (See Fig. 62). In this version the man has the same front facing stance with legs apart and feet turned out. But on the tankard, one of his hands is placed on his waist while the other holds a lance. He now has a hat on his head and puffed out sleeves with a tight-fitting, flared coat. On his feet, he has high heel shoes. The background area is again filled with non-connected geometric designs and animals. On the front of this tankard is a portrait with a head and shoulders, enclosed in a frame and surrounded with non-connected designs.[287] The two examples on the tankard correlate very closely with the manner in which the Father's and Mother's stones were created.

The tankard depicts two styles by which a person's image could be portrayed. The first is a free standing gentleman like on the Father's stone. The second style is to have the head and shoulders enclosed by a frame like the image on the Mother's stone. In addition, the two styles were used side by side on the same tankard. Again, the same scenario Mullicken used when he set up his two stones. Both of these styles were in common usage as folk art motifs during the early 1700's.

Mullicken in carving the Father's stone used a similar face to the one on the Mother's stone. However, the workmanship of the facial features improved and became more human like. The bottom of the nose is rounded and shaped instead of rectangular. The mouth is a solid line

---

[285] Stillinger, 1972: 34.
[286] Stillinger, 1972: 32.
[287] Stillinger, 1972: 91.

verses dots. The hair is even on both sides of the face and on the head is placed a broad-brimmed hat to distinguish the male figure from the female on the Mother's stone.

The gentleman is attired in a tight fitting coat, buttoned down the front with a flared skirt and full sleeves. At the neck under the face is a falling band. The legs are rudimentary with tight pants and high heel shoes. In every detail of the attire, Mullicken duplicates the gentleman on the mug except for some slight changes he made to reflect colonial dress. American naïve paintings c 1700 – 1730 show the same traits, full figure, faced forward with feet spread out and a hand on the hip like the fathers stone. Classic poses for the time period.[288]

The carving is a little out of proportion, especially the short legs. Mullicken, being a rural, self-taught artist may have misjudged the length of the legs. He was accustomed to working with faces on gravestones not with full figures.

To finish the stone, he formatted it after the 1690 doorstone. In each corner there is a circle and on the bottom a triangle is placed under the figure (See Fig. 71). The circles with a dot in the middle were derived from the circles on the 1690 doorstone but were modified by eliminating the inner circle. One means of identifying Mullicken's work are his circles. He has a tendency to carve an uneven "v" groove with one side at a sharp angle and the other slanted (See Fig. 72). Circles on both the Mother's and Father's stones are identical.

Under the figure there is a triangle. The placement of it comes from the 1690 doorstone and the style of it from the 1708 milestone, both carved by John Hartshorn. On the milestone Hartshorn used a free standing double triangle repeated inside of itself and oriented downward (See Fig. 9). On the Father's stone Mullicken carved the same free standing triangle and oriented it downward. However, he modified the design by dropping the inner triangle (See Fig. 73). This is the same modification that he made on the circles. Then he placed the triangle on the bottom edge between two circles like on the 1690 doorstone and incised a line underneath it.

The circles with a dot in the middle are a direct link with the Mother's stone. The triangle forms a link to the Dummer family. The identity of the gentleman on the Father's stone is traced through the complex set of clues left by Mullicken to identify the people represented by the Mother's and Father's stones. He used the gravestones of soldiers in 1723 in Newbury to

---

[288] American Federation of Arts, 1969: 1, 2, 5.

show the gentleman on the Father's stone was a military officer.[289] Captain Richard Dummer, Jr. was one of only two members of his family to obtain a military rank. Furthermore, Captain Richard Dummer had the same high military rank of other men that Mullicken had set apart through symbolism on his 1722 gravestones in Bradford that he had done one year prior to the Father's stone.

The other military officer, in the family was Richard, Jr.'s son, Nathaniel (1685 - 1767), who became a lieutenant about 1724. However, Nathaniel never owned the original farm and mansion house. He was given a section of land at the falls, from his brother, John in lieu of a cash payment. This land later became known as the Fatherland Farm.[290]

---

[289] For a complete discussion of all the information used to identify the Father's Stone please refer to the section on the Mother's Stone.
[290] Watkins, 1969: 27.

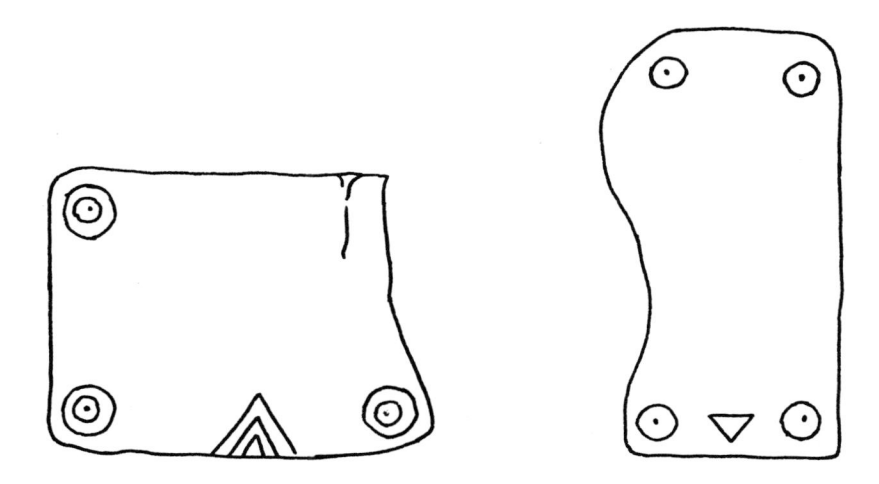

Fig. 71 – A comparison of the layout of the circles and triangle on the 1690 doorstone (left) and the Father's stone (right).

Fig. 72 – A cross-sectional view of the type of groove Robert Mullicken Sr. used when he carved hard diorite stones.

Fig. 73 – John Hartshorn's double triangle from the 1708 milestone (left) compared to Robert Mullicken Sr.'s single triangle from the Father's stone (right).

The Milestones in Newbury

Introduction

In 1707, the first milestones in New England were erected by Judge Samuel Sewall on Newbury Street (now Washington Street) in Boston.[291] During the next three years, dated milestones were erected on the Bay Road in Newbury, Ipswich and Wenham which continued to be the main route used along the coast.[292]

Recognizing that milestones served as points of reference in a day's journey, towns, taverns, and individuals erected them in prominent places. For tavern owners, a nearby milestone served as an aid in advertising their business.[293] In one town, they became show pieces, one being erected in front of the meeting house and carved with a Biblical inscription. Prominent members of the community also had milestones erected and carved with their names or initials.[294] By 1764, milestones became common place when Benjamin Franklin marked the miles off on the postal roads because letters sent via the postal service were charged according to mileage.[295]

One of the prominent people to have milestones erected was John Dummer of Byfield Parish in Newbury, Massachusetts. He commissioned a total of four milestones over a twenty-five year period (1708 - 1733). These four milestones are unique in that they are carved with artistic geometric and symbolic art designs. This is the only known use of these designs on milestones in New England.[296] The symbolic art was comprised of geometric shapes common in colonial decorative arts of the period. The symbolism comes from the fact they were used to form a link with the Dummer family.

---

[291] Wood, 1919: 147.
[292] Jewett, Jewett, 1946.
[293] Earle 1901: 351.
[294] Wood, 1919: 147, 161.
[295] Sloane, 1956: 171-172.
[296] Milestone 20 has a double ")" on either side, Milestone 20 1/2 has a "~", Milestone 21 has ") " and " (", and milestone 34 has " < " and " > ". Although technically geometric designs they lack the artistic characteristics found on the four Dummer milestones. With the Dummer milestones the geometric art is an integral part of the overall design. The geometric art on milestones 20 1/2 and 21 was not well developed and was used to fill blank spaces on the margins of the stone. With milestone 34, it is questionable whether the "arrows" were meant to be decorative or indicate direction or both. In either case, the "arrows" lack the symbolic and artistic composition of the Dummer milestones.

The Dummer milestones marked a distinct change in social thinking. They were public displays of art, a concept which was abhorred by the early Puritan ministers who sought to ban it through colonial laws. The late 1600's saw the power of Puritan ministers diminish dramatically especially after the Salem witch trials of 1692. With the demise of the power of the Puritan ministers came a dramatic increase in gravestones showing up in the burying grounds. Gravestones with their profuse art work were without question intended for public display. With the Dummer milestones, public displays of art were no longer relegated to the burying ground, they were displayed on the Bay Road, an official road of the Massachusetts Bay Colony.

Fig. 74 – Milestone 33.

Milestone 33

Milestone 33 stands on the grounds of the Governor Dummer Academy in Byfield Parish, Newbury, MA (See Fig. 74). A simple fieldstone with a natural, flat face, it was Byfield's first milestone. Carved in 1708, it was erected only a year after Judge Samuel Sewall had commissioned the Bay Colony's first two milestones.[297] Judge Sewall, who was related to the Dummers, his mother was Jane (Dummer) Sewall, kept close ties with his family in Newbury.[298] John Dummer may have gotten his idea for erecting a milestone from Judge Sewall.

In the year 1708, the date carved on the milestone, John Hartshorn, the gravestone carver, moved from Haverhill and traveled on to Byfield. By 1709, he had resettled in the adjoining town of Rowley.[299] Dating the year Hartshorn actually arrived in Byfield is important for he was the local area's first gravestone carver and the carver of milestone 33. The three earliest surviving gravestones in Byfield are Hartshorn's, carved circa 1708.

Byfield does not appear to have had any stone gravestones erected prior to Hartshorn's arrival. Of the three early gravestones, one is an original and the other two are reproductions of his originals as stated on the back by family members who had the new stones carved. The original gravestone, done for Elisabeth [Dummer] Hale, who died in 1704, was carved with a high peaked design over the head that appears on other Hartshorn stones from 1707/8. Elizabeth, the daughter of Richard and Elizabeth Dummer, was John Dummer's sister and the wife of the first Byfield minister, Reverend Moses Hale.

The designs on the reproductions are characteristic of a transition period in Hartshorn's designs which occurred between 1708 and 1710. One design feature went from bars without segments to segmented lines, a significant change that he did not revert back to afterwards (See Fig. 75). Joshuah Woodman, Jr.'s gravestone dated 1706, carved circa 1708 is a good example of the transition. His stone has non-segmented bars, last used in the year 1708, and a design that looks like layered feathers.[300] The layered pattern transitioned into the segmented line seen on Joshuah Woodman's 1703 stone, carved circa 1709/10. At this point Hartshorn also began to

---

[297] Wood, 1919: 147.
[298] Ewell, 1904: 80-81.
[299] Tucker, 1992: 24-25.
[300] Slater, Tucker, Farber, 1978: 138.

incorporate circled designs in the lunette, like the six-pointed rosette on Joshuah's stone. Another feature, that is characteristic of his stones from this period are the designs above the head that disappeared after 1710. Because gravestones were often backdated, these design changes help to establish the actual carving date of the gravestone. The carving date of Elizabeth Hale and Joshuah Woodman, Jr. along with the fact Hartshorn traveled south when he left Haverhill places him in Byfield in 1708.

Fig. 75 – Transition of style in Hartshorn's decorative lines in the lunette: Undulated (left) Segmented (Right).

Another change in Hartshorn's work shows up in the wording which occurred a few years after he started. The majority of his stones have only pertinent information while others were carved with elaborate wording, an indication he worked in conjunction with some of his customers. This openness to work with his customers shows up in milestone 33 and the 1690 doorstone.

Milestone 33 was incised with "N5", "B33", the year "1708" and a double triangle. The information was separated using dividing lines a style observed on other milestones carved between 1708 and 1710 along the Bay Road (See Fig. 76). The carved numbers and letters are large and bold. They are not perfect but do show Hartshorn had command of his work.

The double triangle below the date is a study in itself. This free standing, single design was totally out of the ordinary for Hartshorn. He always filled every inch of the lunette with connected designs on his gravestones. The fact that he allotted space for this triangle and specifically placed it, by itself in the same position as the bar of triangles on the 1636 doorstone, is highly suggestive this design has symbolic meaning. The triangles found on both the 1636 doorstone and milestone 33 have several features in common (See Fig. 77). Each is oriented downward, repeated inside itself and centered under the date. To create his double triangle design, Hartshorn modified the doorstone's design and transferred it to the milestone. Borrowing and modifying a design like this was familiar to him, using it to make a symbolic family connection was a concept new to him. This concept set the precedence for the future use of symbolism on the six Dummer stones to come.

One of those was a doorstone that Hartshorn carved a year later, on which he shows he knew exactly what he was doing with the triangle design. The 1690 doorstone also, has a set of triangles repeated inside of itself. These are the only two examples of triangles he used, none show up on his gravestones.

This link to the 1690 doorstone is one of three important pieces of evidence which identify John Hartshorn as the carver. The designs on the top surface of the 1690 doorstone include a circle design which has been clearly identified as his work.[301] The second piece of evidence is how the "8" was formed on milestone 33. Hartshorn consistently used two circles to form his "8" which is the same way the "8" on the milestone is created. Robert Mullicken Sr., who started carving a few years later, always made his number "8" with a flat top and a circle on the bottom. (Fig. 78) The third piece of evidence is the fact that Hartshorn was present in the Byfield area in 1708.

---

[301] See the 1690 Doorstone for a detailed explanation.

Stories Carved in Stone

Fig. 76 – 1710 Milestone on Route 1A in front of Town Hall in Wenham, MA.
"N" – Newbury
"B" – Boston
"I" – Ipswich
"S" – Salem

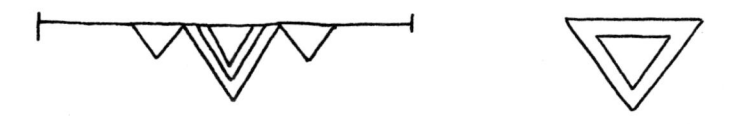

Fig. 77 – Comparison of 1636 Doorstone triangle design (left) & 1708 Milestone triangle (Right)

Fig. 78 – Comparison of John Hartshorn's number eight formed with two circles (left) and Robert Mullicken Sr.'s number eight with flat top (right).

Fig. 79 – Fragment of Milestone 34.

Milestone 34

In 1997, near the mile 34 mark on Middle Road (old Bay Road), part of a "1710" style milestone was dug up when an old stone wall was being rebuilt (See Fig. 79). Although milestone 34 is not part of the Dummer stone collection, it contributes significantly to our understanding of stone carving in the early 1700's. Milestone 34 was one of six milestones between Wenham and Byfield on the Bay Road carved between 1708 and 1710.[302] These early milestones came at a transition period in the decorative arts. They are some of the earliest public displays of carved art (except for gravestones). The designs are simple and conservative. These designs would become bold and prolific a little over twenty years later as was witnessed by milestones 35, 36, 37.

The middle section of milestone 34 is the only portion that has been recovered. The stone is a hard granite possibly diorite. The fragment measures approximately 14 inches wide by 16 inches tall and varies from 6 inches to 8 inches in thickness. The stone has a natural flat face that was carved on. The carving consists of the letters "N" and "B", the numbers 4 and 34, two designs which look like arrows but may be decoration and vertical and horizontal lines that divide the stone into six equal squares. (The top half of the numbers are missing but sufficient amount is left to positively identify the numbers) The two bottom squares contain two "V" shaped "arrows", one in each square, which point left and right respectively. The method used to carve the lines on this stone was a shallow square groove.

The "4" and the "N" stand for four miles to Newbury (measured to the center of town, at the upper green) and "34" and "B" stand for thirty-four miles to Boston. The fragment was found on the west side of the road in an old stone wall. However, originally it would have stood on the opposite or east side of the road. (In order for the milestone to point in the right direction to both towns, Newbury to the north and Boston to the south, it needed to be positioned facing the road on the east side. In this position the left side with "N 4" points to the north and the right side with "B 34" points to the south.) This position is consistent with the rest of the surviving milestones found along the Bay Road which were designed to be placed on the east side of the

---

[302] Jewett & Jewett, 1946: 159-161.

road.[303] In 2002, a small granite marker was placed at the approximate location Milestone 34 would have stood.

Milestone 34 has many similarities with milestones "20", "20 1/2" and "21" in Wenham (all dated 1710) and milestone "33" in Byfield (dated 1708). Milestone 34 would have stood from 2 to 3 feet above the ground which is the same height as the above mentioned milestones. All five milestones contain vertical and horizontal lines which divide the information. The use of lines to divide the information was not used on milestones dated after 1710. Based upon this evidence, it is concluded that milestone 34 was carved circa 1710.

Milestone 34 has the same post like shape as the Wenham milestones. Milestone 33 in Byfield is shaped like a half circle. Milestone 34, however, differs from the Wenham milestones in one major way. As fig. 80 illustrates, it follows the "mileage over the town" format of Milestone 33 not the "town over the mileage" format of the Wenham milestones. To complicate matters more, Milestone 34 places the mileage and the town into separate boxes instead of keeping them in the same box like on the Wenham milestones and Milestone 33. Milestone 34 is not an exact copy of any of the Wenham milestones or milestone 33. Furthermore, it adds the new feature of separating the mileage and town into individual boxes. This suggests that milestone 34 was carved by someone other than the people who carved Milestones 20, 20 1/2, 21 and 33.

Fig. 80 - Position of "Mileage" and "Town" on the Milestones

	"20", "20 1/2", "21"	"33"	"34"
TOP	Town	Mileage	Mileage
BOTTOM	Mileage	Town	Town

Milestone 34 was carved with a shallow square groove. This type of groove suggests that the carver had little or no training in stone carving. Professional stone carvers from this time period used a "V" shaped groove on their work not the shallow square groove found on this

---
[303] Jewett & Jewett, 1946: 162.

stone. The shallow nature of the groove also indicates a lack of skill by the stone carver. Professional carvers cut a much deeper groove even on hard granite. The shallowness may also indicate a lack of proper tools for this type of work. The square groove is similar to square cuts found in "tongue and groove" woodworking. The carver may have been a carpenter. This possibility is supported further by the fact that the lines are carved straight and with an even width. The lettering is of uniform height, width and well laid out. Although the carver lacked the skills and techniques of the professional stone carvers, he had a steady hand and the basic skills to use carving tools.

On this milestone the letter "B" has an unusual shape (See Fig. 81). This style "B" is not found on any gravestones or milestones dating from 1700 to 1750. A close inspection of the letter "B" shows that its "unusual" shape was probably an attempt to cover up a mistake. The rough, ragged edges of the grooves that form the middle loop (the unusual shape) of this letter indicate the carving tool was dull. Dull tools have a tendency to slip. The letter "B" is also missing its bottom serif. All of this indicates, once again, the carver's lack of experience with stone carving.

Fig. 81 - Milestone 34, the letter "B"

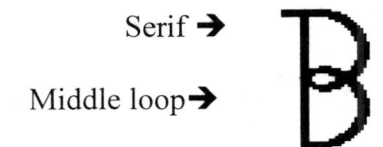

Serif →

Middle loop →

The final item which needs to be discussed is the two "arrows". The "arrows" may have been meant to indicate direction or they may be decorative or a combination of both. The Wenham stones and Milestone 33, all contain minor added decorative details. Milestone 34's "arrows" most closely resemble the decorative curved line design on Milestone 21 (See Fig. 82). On Milestones 20 and 21 there are curved lines in each of the top corners that form half circles facing outward. Milestones 20, 21 and 33 also have other features worth noting. Milestone 20 has a Biblical quotation, 21 has the initials "D D" and 33 has a double triangle. The double triangle is a symbolic representation from a design found on an earlier Dummer doorstone.[304] The initials "D D" on milestone 21 are most likely those of the person who commissioned the stone (See Fig. 83). This became a more common practice later in the eighteenth century, as indicated by a milestone inscribed with "B 4, 1735, P D". The initials "P D" stand for Paul Dudley.[305] All five of the milestones have both similarities and individualities which appear to be common for the time period.

Wenham's milestones have one other distinction they appear to have been prestigious show pieces as indicated by Milestone 20. (Fig. 84) On this milestone a verse from the Bible was carved. It was appropriately chosen for its location which happened to be in front of the meeting house and burying ground. The verse on the stone reads, "I know that tho wilt bring me to death, and to the house ~ appointed for all living."[306] Passersby would have made the association with "the house appointed for all living" and those attending the meeting, as well as "bring me to death" and the burying ground. On the knoll behind this milestone, which is cemented into the stone wall, is an old burying ground. In there, the older gravestones form a three sided square around the area where the old meeting house once stood. After the old meeting house disappeared the land was reclaimed by the cemetery and used for newer graves.

Milestone 34 was located across the River Parker from the Dummer family owned lands. In no way does it resemble the work of the carvers John Hartshorn or the Mullicken family, who John Dummer employed. It does show strong evidence of having been carved circa 1710. Who commissioned it and the actual carving date are unknown. However, circumstantial evidence indicates it was the original Milestone 34 to be erected on this spot.

Milestone 34 was erected on the Sewall family side of the River Parker on the country road. No connection has been documented between this milestone and the Sewall family. However, it is likely they had it erected as a monument on their side of the river. The rivalry between the Dummer family and themselves, over the naming of the Byfield parish, suggests this as a likely scenario.[307] No other milestones existed in the town of Newbury until three more were erected twenty years later in the mid 1730's.

---

[304] See Milestone 33 for a detailed explanation.
[305] Wood, 1919: 147, 161.
[306] Job 30:23 - King James version.
[307] See the complete discussion of this under the "Third Generation" chapter.

Stories Carved in Stone

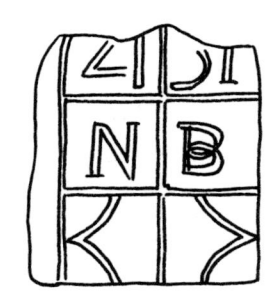

Fig. 82 – Milestone 21 and 34 with their respective designs.

Fig. 83 – Milestone 21 on Route 1A in Wenham, MA. (Left)
Fig. 84 – Milestone 20 on Route 1A in Wenham, MA. (Right)

Fig. 85 – Milestone 35.

Milestone 35

When the Mullicken's created milestones 35, 36 and 37, they used the basic layout found on the 1636 doorstone. This formed a unique symbolic pattern that connected each milestone to the Dummer family. It consists of a pair of designs, year and a repeated pattern of designs on a line beneath it. On the doorstone this layout is represented by the fleur-de-lis on each side of the year and the line of triangles underneath it. In the Mullickens version on the milestones, they chose circles as a replacement design for the fleur-de-lis on the doorstone. In place of the year the number of miles from Boston was carved along with the letter "B." For the bottom line of triangles, they replaced it with designs that reflected each carver's style at the time.

Milestone 35 has a pair of pie shaped circles with scalloped edges, the letter B, the number 35 and a line of triangles (See Fig. 85). The mileage, "35" is oversized for the designs but neatly incised, though not deeply cut. The "B" for Boston, shows the characteristic trademark of the Mullicken family with its elongated serifs. The design under the mileage is a line of repeated, single triangles oriented downward. It shows a similarity to the repeated triangle pattern on the 1636 doorstone.[308] Yet the design has its own unique pattern used only on this stone.

Of all the milestones, Milestone 35 is the only one that shows a clear command of composition. The composition is balanced and well throughout. Stylistically, there is a strong sense of continuity between the circle design at the top and the triangle design at the bottom. The designs have a simple elegance which compliments the shape of the stone. In the same way that the designs compliment the stone, the shape of the stone compliments the landscape. It is located at the edge of open farmland (corner of Middle & Boston Roads) were it stands just high enough to be easily viewed but it doesn't overpower the surrounding landscape. The workmanship is the work of an accomplished stone carver, the composition is the work of artistic mind. The carver was John Mullicken.

---

[308] Amongst the papers on file at the Byfield Public Library is a manuscript page with three drawings on it. The page is titled "Drawings made from rocks on the Newbury Poor Farm in South Byfield." It shows the 1640 doorstone, a second stone with a triangle & half circle pattern, and a third stone with a triangle pattern on the edge similar to milestone 35. This stone was reported to have been found in the leanto under the wall at the Poor Farm [Former Dummer Farm at the Falls]. Its relationship to milestone 35 is not known, especially since it can not be dated. It is impossible to determine if Mullicken took the design for the 35 milestone from this stone. This manuscript page was part of the Stephen Hale papers. See Appendix D.

In Belleville Cemetery, Newburyport (formerly Newbury until 1764) there is a gravestone by John Mullicken done for Mr. Samuel Bartlett dated 1732. This grave's footstone is the key factor in connecting John with Milestone 35. The footstone is carved with an unusual line of three fleurs-de-lis given to Mr. Bartlett telling people he was an important person, being one of the founders of that parish (See Fig. 86). It is the only example of a repeated pattern on a line, done by him. The footstone has another feature its design was carved using an incised line method. Most of his footstones were carved in this way, which differs from his headstones, showing he worked with the incised line method, too. On Samuel's headstone, he used the flat-raised method, a style that was in use by John from approximately 1731 to 1734.

Fig. 86 – Mr. Samuel Bartlett's 1732 footstone with the incised line of fleur-de-lis. It was carved by John Mullicken. It is located in Belleville Cemetery, Newburyport, MA.

Another gravestone that contributes in dating the milestone has an interesting side border design. On Richard Titcomb's 1736 headstone John used a triangular version of the standard spiral (See Fig. 87). The standard spiral used an "S" shaped, curved line (See Fig. 88). The repeated pattern of the triangular shaped line manifests itself in this side border design like the repeated pattern of triangles on Milestone 35. This headstone overall is a good example of the style he used between 1734 and 1736. It shows designs with simple clean lines and repeated patterns. Note the circle repeated inside itself in the lunette, this simplistic style of design is very similar to that used on the milestone. During this period he, also brought back the molded design on his headstones. An important factor because John used the molded method to carve the double triangle on Milestone 37. All of this evidence places the carving date of Milestone 35 between 1733 and 1735.

Fig. 87 – Richard Titcomb's 1736 headstone with triangular shapes in the side border verses the normally curved lines with spirals (See Fig. 88). It was carved John Mullicken. It is located Old Hill burying ground, Newburyport, MA.

Fig. 88 – Side border with triangular spiral (left). Side border with standard curved spiral (right).

Stories Carved in Stone

Fig. 89 – Milestone 36.

Milestone 36

Milestone 36's narrow shape is radically different from the broad shape of Milestones 33, 35 and 37. Its shape appears to have been carefully chosen to make it standout against the restricted field of vision caused by the sharp curve on Boston road. Its narrow shape gives it the appearance of being a tall stone which solved the visual problem but on the other hand it presented a challenge in terms of creating designs for it. Most of the designs used by the gravestone carvers were created for wide gravestones. Robert Mullicken, Sr., who came out of retirement for this project, met this challenge by creating a new and innovative design.

The stone was originally incised with a single circle design, the number 36, B and a design at the base (See Fig. 89). The top circle (most of which is missing) appears to have been a whorl design. The six in the number 36 was done in the "old style" of the 1600's using a circle with a tail, like the sixes on the doorstones and the uneven "V" groove like the circles on the Father's stone. Robert, Sr. was the only member of his family to carve circles in this manner. The letter "B" has the elongated serifs that the Mullickens used on their gravestones. Completing the stone is a design with a triangle and half circles. This is a complex design drawing on elements from the 1636 doorstone and the Mother's stone. It was a new design created for the sole purpose of this project.[309]

For the milestone design, Robert, Sr. turned the 1636's triangular design upwards and replaced the smaller triangles at both ends with half circles as seen in the frame on the Mother's stone (See Fig. 90). In between the half circles he carved a tall triangle. He repeated the design inside itself in the same manner as the middle triangle on the 1636 doorstone. He then placed a dot in the center on the line in each of the three sections. This dot originates from the circles with a dot in the middle on the 1690, and the Mother's and Father's stones. Then he carved an extra

---

[309] Amongst the papers on file at the Byfield Public Library is a manuscript page with three drawings on it. The page is titled "Drawings made from rocks on the Newbury Poor Farm in South Byfield." It shows the 1640 doorstone, the edge of another stone with a triangle pattern, and a third stone with a pattern similar to the triangle & circle design of milestone 36. This stone was reported to have been found in the foundation of the Poor House [formerly the Dummer Mansion House]. Its relationship to milestone 36 is not known, especially since it can not be dated. It is impossible to determine if Mullicken took the design for the 36 milestone from this stone. This manuscript page was part of the Stephen Hale papers. See Appendix D.

Stories Carved in Stone

line underneath as was done on the bottom of the Father's stone. Each aspect of this complex design is connected to the other Dummer stones that Robert, Sr. had dealt with in the past.

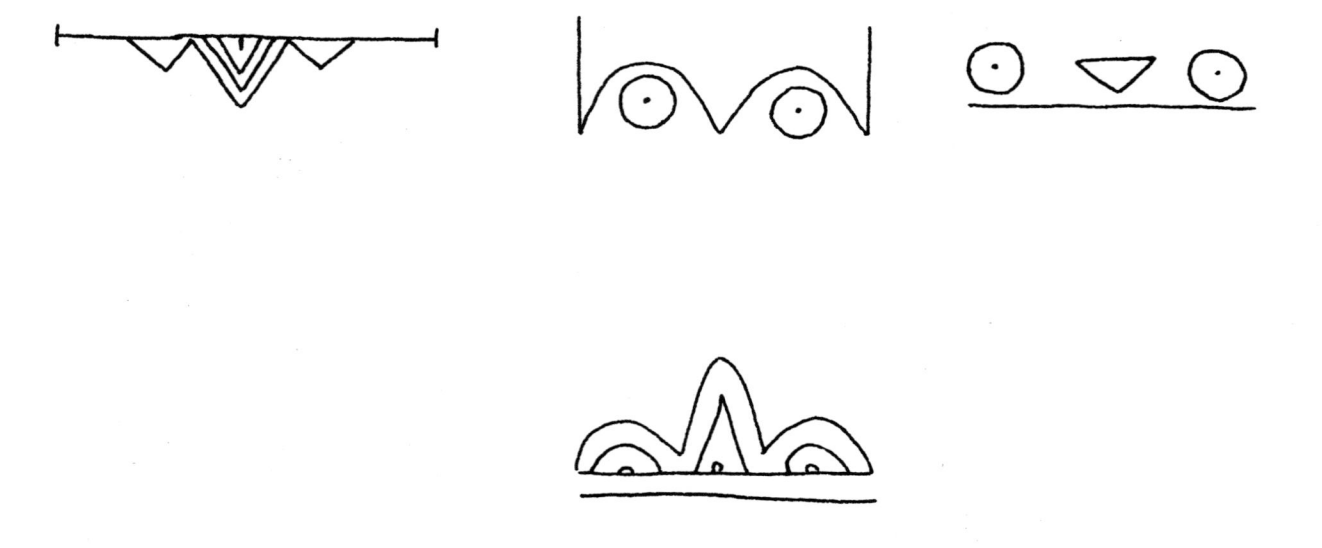

Fig. 90 – Comparison of the various designs found on three of the Dummer stones that may have contributed to the design on milestone 36.

(Top Left) – 1636 doorstone.
(Top Center) – Mother's stone
(Top Right) – Father's stone.
(Bottom Center) – Milestone 36.

Another design that factored in was from a gravestone dated 1727 by Robert, Sr. On it he carved double, multi-lined arches with a tall center line topped off with spirals under the mask like face (See Fig. 91). This was a new concept that used two different designs combined to form a unit under the face. The design incorporated a tall middle portion, balanced on either side by a shorter design which was repeated inside of itself. All three of these factors show up in Milestone 36's design. It was also the last design he introduced before retiring. Variations of the multi-lined arches without the middle design, on this gravestone, were picked up and used by his sons afterwards from 1730 to 1736.

Since Robert, Sr. came out of retirement to carve this stone there is no direct means of dating the stone based on his gravestone work. It is reasonable to assume based on the well established carving dates of Milestones 35 and 37 that it was carved between 1733 and 1735.

Fig. 91 – Captain Hugh March's 1727 headstone with the multi-lined design under the face. It was carved by Robert Mullicken, Sr. It is located in the Bridge Street Cemetery, West Newbury, MA.

Fig. 92 – Milestone 37.

Milestone 37

Milestone 37 attracts the travelers' attention with its bold, opposite whorls (See Fig. 92). A low, wide stone, it stands at the corner of Green and Hanover Streets. It was carved on the front with "B 37", whorls, and a line with arches. On top is a double triangle. One end is marked with "P 26" and a triangle and the other is marked with "I 10."

This stone's significance lies not so much in its bold designs but in its symbolism. The passing traveler was probably completely unaware of it, but, Milestone 37 marked the boundary between two distinctly different social worlds. Located at the end of a field and just short of the upper green, it marked the end of the agricultural farms and the beginning of the urban center growing up around the portside of Newbury at the mouth of the Merrimac River. The double triangle design on the top of Milestone 37 was taken from Milestone 33 and was meant to clearly indicate that this was the end of the series. It is also a direct symbolic link to the Dummers.

Milestone 37 is symbolic in another powerful but very subtle way. It is the collaborative work of all four Mullickens; Robert Sr., Robert Jr., John, and Joseph. It speaks of the strong emphasis placed on family. Joseph, who had only recently begun his apprenticeship as a carver, was included in this important project, in spite of his lack of skill and a steady hand.

The most striking features are the opposite facing whorls. Robert, Jr., who carved the whorls, formed them by carving crescent shaped wedges that are heavily molded. He used this same type of whorl on two of his gravestones in Newbury. Amos Beck's headstone, dated 1735 in Old Hill (Newburyport) has a good example of this opposite whorl style. Beck's headstone also has tall arches, the secondary design in use by Robert, Jr. during 1735/36. Another example is in Sawyers Hill on a stone dated 1733 for Susannah Morss (See Fig. 93). This stone's artwork was carved by Robert, Jr. but lettered by his brother, John (distinguished by the lower case "a"). The artwork has Robert, Jr.'s characteristic crescent shaped whorls (John was using a fan-shaped whorl by 1733) and his tall, two piece design under the face. This joint workmanship occurred on several other occasions and was documented on probate records. There are a few other poorer quality sets of opposite whorls done by a Mullicken apprentice, who was probably Joseph. The whorls are the primary means of dating this milestone. They place the carving date between 1733 and 1735.

Fig. 93 – Mrs. Susannah Morss's 1733 headstone with crescent shaped opposite whorls carved by Robert Mullicken Jr. It is located in Sawyer's Hill Burying Ground, Newburyport, MA.

Fig. 94 – Mrs. Sarah Brown's 1732 headstone with double arches carved Joseph Mullicken as an apprentice. It is located in Sawyer's Hill Burying Ground, Newburyport, MA.

There is a fancy number 37 which is slanted downward with curled-up tips and the regular Mullicken letter "B", both deeply incised. Underneath the mileage is a poorly carved, uneven line with double arches by Joseph. An example of low double arches carved by him is seen on Sarah Brown's 1732 headstone which was lettered by his brother, John (See Fig. 94). The artwork on this gravestone is clearly the work of an apprentice and Joseph was the only one in the shop learning the trade at the time. Currently, the arches on milestone 37 have sunk below ground level and can not be seen.

Whereas Milestones 35 and 36 were the work of a single carver, Milestone 37 was a collaborative effort of all the Mullicken family gravestone carvers. This included Joseph, an adult apprentice at the time. Joseph's inclusion in the project suggests that the project had some importance or significance at the time of its completion. The year 1735 was the centennial of the town of Newbury. The milestone 37 may have commemorated the centennial. Whatever, the purpose, from this humble beginning Joseph went on to be a fine gravestone carver.

On each end, information was given for towns north and south of Newbury. Ipswich to the south was denoted by an "I" with a crossbar, a Mullicken Family trademark and "10" for ten miles. (By this time, the use of the crossbar had been dropped by most carvers.) The other end was carved with "P" for Portsmouth, New Hampshire "26" miles away. The twenty-six was done with an old fashion six made up of a circle with a tail, like Milestone 36. Under the mileage is a single triangle like the one on the Father's stone (See Fig. 95). Its meaning is unknown, however, when Robert, Sr. transferred both the circles and triangles that Hartshorn had originally created, over to the Mother's and Father's stones he dropped the double ones and made single ones. In essence, Robert, Sr. created his own mark to distinguish himself from Hartshorn. It is possible, Robert Sr., who did not sign his stones, made an exception on this, the final important stone of his career.

On the wide top face Milestone 37 is a double triangle repeated inside of itself like the one on Milestone 33 (See Fig. 96). This was carved by John using his smooth, rounded-off method (See Fig. 97). The refined, neatly carved triangle compliments the boldly, molded whorls. The double triangle marks the final stone in the series, the first being Milestone 33 with its own double triangle. Furthermore, it links the milestones to the Dummer family.

Fig. 95 – End of Milestone 37 with "P 26" and a single triangle carved by Robert Mullicken Sr.

Fig. 96 – Double triangle on the narrow top side of milestone 37 carved by John Mullicken.

Fig. 97 – Close-up of finial design with the smooth rounded finish of John Mullicken. It is on Elizabeth Huse's 1734 headstone carved by John. It is located in Sawyer's Hill Burying Ground, Newburyport, MA.

Conclusion

The Dummer carved stones of Newbury, Massachusetts mirror the greater picture of the rural gravestone carver's work and an upper class family's inheritance of the land. Although "primitive" by modern standards, the artwork demonstrates a sophisticated thought process in the use of symbolism. From its inception this art was used to make social statements, used as decoration and used to form a link with the Dummer family. One of the first stones, the 1636 doorstone, embodied all three factors, which were brought over from England. However, the concept was new, for it was a compilation on a single entity of designs which had always been used separately on English houses at the time.

Richard Dummer, Sr. attracted by prospects of vast tracts of land, came to New England to build. Land was a commodity he valued above money. In Newbury, he found his opportunity to establish an estate and the Dummer family. Once he was firmly established on his Newbury farm, he commissioned the second of two doorstones. The unique, decorated 1636 doorstone was a product of Dummer's creativity. It was a means to display his armorial symbol on his land and estate, like in England. Dummer had transplanted himself from England to New England to obtain land not to get away from British customs. He attempted to recreate in Newbury, what he left in Bishopstoke. His 1636 doorstone even has pure decoration, like those used on house roofs back in England. The doorstone was a symbol, representative of his acquiring land on which he could build and expand to create a manor farm. This symbolic doorstone set the precedence for his grandson, John and the gravestone carver's art that was to follow.

Art was an important part of this family's heritage in New England. Richard, Sr.'s second son, Jeremiah received an apprenticeship with a well established silversmith instead of college like his brother, Shubael. Each were costly for Richard, so undoubtedly Jeremiah, who was an artist in his own right, must have shown some talent at a young age. Jeremiah became a well known silversmith and an unknown portrait painter. There are four known portraits signed by him and two more attributed to him but unsigned.[310]

When Richard, Sr. died in 1679, the family had a gravestone incised for him. The gravestone was a rare commodity at the time in the colony and even rarer beyond the Boston and

Salem town limits. Three years later, in 1682, Richard's wife, Frances Dummer died and she too had a gravestone ordered for her. There are only two other gravestones dated 1674 and 1679, both are the same style of plain stone accorded Frances and Richard Dummer. These were the precursors of the decorated slate gravestones of Boston which began to arrive in Newbury in 1686.

Frances' gravestone had to have been purchased by her son, Richard Dummer, Jr. Although he used a different method, Richard, Jr. continued to use stone as a marker. In this case, he went out of his way to obtain a gravestone. Not only that, before it was stylish, he had a stone marker placed on a woman's grave. The Dummer men had a great deal of respect for the women in their family. In 1689, Richard, Jr. died and his wife, Elizabeth followed suit. She had a distinct advantage, a connection in Boston, her brother-in-law Jeremiah, who may have aided her in purchasing a stylish Boston decorated carved gravestone for her husband. Elizabeth got the best gravestone available at the time which was no small feat. These three gravestones were amongst the earliest in Newbury's burying grounds. The Dummer's who procured them had to have gone out of their way to do so. From early on it was evident that stone markers were important to this family. Within a few years, other town's people followed suit and ordered gravestones for their family members.

John Dummer of the third generation was a witness to his family's use of stone markers. He was six when his grandmother died and thirteen at the death of his father, old enough to realize the importance of these stone markers, which interested and intrigued him. On top of that, John inherited his Uncle Jeremiah's love of art and his grandfather's sense of reverence for family, land, and heritage. However, John went to local gravestone carvers to create masterpieces for his stones.

Primarily self-taught, the local gravestone carvers were from the middle class and were already a master craftsman of another trade. They were independent small businessmen, who supplemented their income by plying a second trade. The first two carvers, who were weavers, had to learn from scratch, how to quarry their stone, carve, letter and create designs. Neither had the chance to apprentice with a master carver, although the second had the advantage of some advise and designs from the first. These two were the ones who set the example and precedence

---

[310] Phillips, 1945: 41.

for those who followed them. They were creative and innovative with a great sense of pride in their work. No detail escaped their bright and intelligent minds in an effort to update the ideas and designs on their gravestones, as well as find ways to create their masterpieces.

The first, Hartshorn, who had not been exposed to the Boston style, developed the Merrimac Valley Style and the second, Mullicken, carried it on, just like the Boston carvers did, one generation to the next. Each carver, in turn, eventually added his own touch and thereby created his own signature. That signature gave each carver his own identity, which appears to be personal rather than professional, for in the case of Hartshorn and Mullicken, they did not compete for business. The two of them had separate territories where they sold their stones during the time they both lived in the Merrimac Valley.

The carvers in a quest to improve their work and be more professional kept themselves abreast of current worldly trends, making it into their areas. These trends manifested themselves in the gravestone art. In some cases they were subtle and others, clear and concise, however, frequent design changes, to better their work, made them short lived.

John Hartshorn and Robert Mullicken, Sr.'s gravestone art is a microcosm of the early eighteenth century thoughts. Art was becoming art for arts sake, as seen in the designs used in conjunction with the various types of faces and skulls. Women, whose untold stories helped shape this new colony, were expounded upon and honored through art and inscriptions, and men, whose intelligence and integrity earned them a high military rank were likewise set apart through art. Art as in eons past was a medium to convey what was going on in society. The Dummer's stones brought this art form to its greatest height.

John Dummer's love of art and his fascination with his grandfather's doorstones conveying art and heritage fostered a unique group of highly decorated carved stones. His milestones and doorstones encouraged and challenged the gravestone carvers to stretch their minds to find ways to carry on the ideas embodied in the 1636 doorstone.

Hartshorn started the sequence of symbolic art by modifying an existing design on the 1636 doorstone and transferring it to the 1708 milestone. Robert Mullicken, Sr. went on to bring this symbolism to its height through the artwork on the Mother's stone, where he speaks of Elizabeth Dummer's love, respect and dedication. In the eyes of her family she was a loving mother, the protector of the land and a dedicated wife. Elizabeth Dummer was immortalized in stone by her son and the stone carver.

This knowledge, like Richard Dummer, Sr.'s land was passed on to sons. Robert Mullicken, Sr., became the teacher, of his sons, Robert Jr., John and Joseph. Together they created the milestones, the culmination of their collaborative artwork. A significant achievement, in that the Mullicken's individually and collectively, brought their talents together in this project. With no two stones alike, they created original and unmistakable designs that form a link with the 1636 doorstone. This ended, with the triumphant Milestone 37, so brilliantly mastered. Through the milestone art, the Mullicken's linked the past with the present and John Dummer's desire to preserve a way of life.

Robert's sons followed in their father's footsteps. Robert, Jr. became the patient teacher, John mastered the art and using a sculptured look he brought the original Merrimac Valley Style to its height, Joseph's creativeness expanded upon both style and the tradition of acknowledging women, in time he honored women on their gravestones by placing a bonnet about the face in the lunette.

We are indebted to these early gravestone carvers, whose insight and knowledge of the world around them, found its way into their artwork. And to the Dummer's, whose love and respect of land, family and heritage, brought us the carved stones.

Stories Carved in Stone

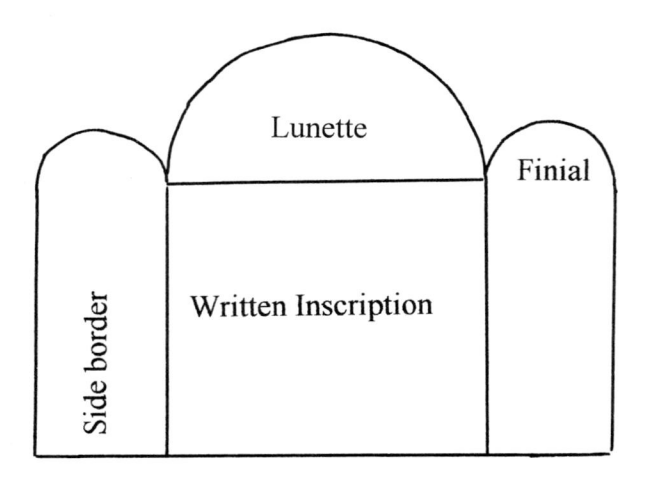

Fig. 98 – Parts of the gravestone.

Glossary

Banded - A wide band encircling a design.

Cherub - An angle like face with human features and often carved with wings.

Finials - Small rounded corners on either side of the lunette at the top of the head or footstone.

Fanned out - A wide design beginning with a thin side flush with the background that ends in a thin raised side much higher than it starting point.

Fleur-de-lis - Heraldic symbol which represents the iris flower.

Footstone - Small stone placed at the foot of a grave.

Headstone - Large stone at the head of a grave with the person's name and date of death.

Incised line - A "V' shaped grooved line used for both lettering and designs.

Lunette - The semi-circular space at the top of the headstone that was carved with designs.

Mask like face - A simple semi-rounded shaped face with round eyes, linear nose and mouth.

Molded - A raised, rounded off design that has a smooth looking finish.

Non-connected - Free standing designs in the lunette; designs that are not attached or physically linked together with other elements in the lunette.

Raised - This method raises the design above the background surface; it can have a flat top with straight sides or be semi-rounded.

Secondary - Smaller designs used to fill the areas in the lunette around the large circled designs and face.

Segmented line - Horizontal lines used to connect two curved parallel lines in the lunette.

Side border - Wide vertical space on both sides of the epitaph carved with designs.

Slab-top tombstone - A very large, flat stone the size of a coffin that was placed directly over the grave either on the ground or on blocks above it

Undulating line - A wide or narrow line with smooth wave like curves.

Whorls - Pin-wheel like design.

Appendix A - Gravestones used in this Study

Death Date	Date Carved	Name of Deceased	Cem.	Carver	Symbol(s)	Headstone / Footstone
1698	(1706)	John Rolfe	H	JH	Circles	H
1699		John Rolfe [Jr. ?]				
1700		Captain Daniel Wicom	R	JL	Slate / skull design	H
1701		Colonel Pierce	FP	Boston	2 F-D-L	S
1703		Mary Hasalthine	H	JH	Early Hartshorn example	H
1705	(1709)	Sara Wicom	R	JH	Crown	H
1708		Sari Buswell	S	JH	Circles	H
1708		Mary Sawyer	SH	JH	Hearts in side border 2 F-D-L	H F
1708		Mary Baily	SH	JH	Example footstone design	F
1709		Insigne Henery Lunt	FP	JH	Circles	H
1709		Sargent Samuel Gill	S	JH	Circles	H
1712		Sara Safford	I	JH	Example MVR style	H
1715		--------- -----------	B	RMSr	Hearts beside head (No circles)	H
1715		Joseph Palmer	B	RMSr	2 F-D-L beside head (No circles)	H
1717		Major Daniel Davison	FP	Boston	Cherub's head	H
1718		John ---------------	H	RMSr	1 F-D-L Botom. graffiti "Josep"	H
1718		Sargent John Ordway	SH	RMSr	Stars	H
1718		Lt. Samuel Sawyer	SH	RMSr	Star over head	H
1719		Dorkes Bartlet	SH	RMSr	1 F-D-L & Stars	H
1719		----- ---crocker	H	RMSr	1 F-D-L	H
1720		Samuel Mulicken	B	RMSr	1 F-D-L	H
1721		Mary Carlton	B	RMSr	2 F-D-L (apprentice's work)	F
1721		Captain Nathanael Walker	B	RMSr	Skull	H

Date carved is the date the stones were actually carved verses the date of death. If no date is listed in this column then the stones were carved in the same year as the death date.

Death Date	Date Carved	Name of Deceased	Cem.	Carver	Symbol(s)	Headstone / Footstone
1722		Captain Philip Attwood	B	RMSr	Skull 3 F-D-L	H F
1722		Abigail Sawyer	SH	RMSr	1 F-D-L	H
1723		Samuel Sawyer	SH	RMSr	2 F-D-L	H
1723		John Sawyer	SH	RMSr	2 Hearts 2 F-D-L	H F
1723		Insign Benjamin Smith	SH	RMSr	2 F-D-L	F
1723		Ensign Joseph Knight	FP	RMSr	2 F-D-L 2 F-D-L	H F
1723		John Knight	SH	RMSr	2 Hearts	H
1724		John Brown	FP	RMSr	2 Hearts	H
1725		Mary Little	SH	RMJr	2 Hearts	F
1725		Aphya Coffin	FP	John	Low arches	H
1726		Issac Bayliy	SH	RMSr	2 Hearts	F
1726		Nicolas Colby	FP	John	Early Design	H
1727		Capt. Hugh March	WN	RMSr	Multi-lined arches	H
1727	(1729)	Tristram Coffin	FP	John	Molded design	H
1727		Sarah Bartlett	BE	John	1 heart	H
1728	(1730)	Benaiah Titcom	FP	John	Flat-raised design	H
1728	(1732)	Abigail Allen	FP	RMJr	Incised line secondary designs	H
1728		Maray Grffing	B	RMJr	2 F-D-L	F
1728		Hannah Woodman	B	RMJr	Opposite whorls	H
1729		Hannah Ayers	H	RMJr	2 Hearts by Joseph (apprentice at time)	H
1729		Sarah Foster	SC	John	Opposite Whorls	H
1729		James White	H	RMJr	Opposite Whorls	H
1729		Lydia Greffen	B	John	Opposite Whorls	H
1730		Jonathan Woodman	FP	RMJr	2 Hearts w/design inside	H
?	(1730)	Unknown	OH	RMJr	2 Hearts w/design inside	H
1732		Sarah Brown	SH	Joseph	Arches	H
1732		Edna Little	SH	RMJr	2 Hearts	H
1732		Samuel Bartlett	BE	John	3 F-D-L	F
1733		Susannah Morss	SH	RMJr	Opposite whorls	H
1733		John Stickney	FP	John	Fan-shaped whorls	H
1734		John Huse & 19 Day old brother	SH	RMJr	Arch	H

Date carved is the date the stones were actually carved verses the date of death. If no date is listed in this column then the stones were carved in the same year as the death date.

Stories Carved in Stone

Death Date	Date Carved	Name of Deceased	Cem.	Carver	Symbol(s)	Headstone / Footstone
1734		Elizabeth Huse	SH	John	Repeated Circles	H
1735		Amos Beck	OH	RMJr	Opposite whorls & arches	H
1736		Elisabeth Mtthard	H	RMJr	Opposite whorls	H
1736		John Huse	SH	RMJr	Examples of circles on footstone	F
1736		Richard Titcomb	OH	John	Diagonal side border design	H
1736		Jonathan Colby	M	Joseph	Early example of his work	H
1737		Mehetabel Savage	OH	John	2 Hearts with wide band	H
?	(1736)	John Greenleuf	FP	RMJr	2 Hearts with wide band	H
1747		Anna Rogers	SH	Joseph	Example shows John's influence	H
1757		Susannah Burbank	G	Joseph	Bonnet	H

Date carved is the date the stones were actually carved verses the date of death. If no date is listed in this column then the stones were carved in the same year as the death date.

LEGEND

Carvers

JH - John Hartshorn
JL - Joseph Lamson
RMSr - Robert Mullicken, Sr
RMJr - Robert Mullicken, Jr.
John - John Mullicken
Joseph - Joseph Mullicken
Boston - Professional Stone carvers of Boston

Gravestone design explanation

F-D-L - Fleur- de-lis
H - Headstone
F - Footstone
S - Slab tombstone

Burying Grounds (See Appendix "C")

B - Bradford Burying Ground: Bradford, MA
BE - Belleville: Newburyport, MA
FP - First Parish, Newbury: MA
G - Riverview, Groveland: MA
H - Pentucket Burying Ground: Haverhill, MA
I - Old Burying Ground: Ipswich, MA
M - Church Street Cemetery: Merrimac, MA
OH - Old Hill: Newburyport, MA
R - Rowley Burying Ground: Rowley, MA
S - First Cemetery: Salisbury, MA
SH - Sawyers Hill: Newburyport, MA
SC - South Church: Andover, MA
WN - Bridge Street: West Newbury, MA

NOTES: For the sake of clarity, only gravestones that were used as evidence in this study were included. There are several noticeable emissions from this list. These omissions should not be construed to imply that they contradict the arguments present in this study. The majority of the evidence is based on which variation of the design was used and the technique used to carve it, not on its use in general. They include:

1. Only a partial list of Robert Mullicken Sr.'s gravestones which have a single fleur-de-lis design.
2. Only a partial list of Robert Jr. and John Mullicken's gravestones which have hearts or fleur-de-lis designs on them.

***For more information on the gravestones of individual carvers please consult:

Hartshorn - (Slater, Tucker, Farber, 1978) - Provides a complete list of stones.
Mullickens - (Tucker, 1992) - Provides a statistical overview of their stones with selected examples. Please contact the Association for Gravestone Studies, Worcester MA. for a complete list of stones. Consult the phonebook or their internet homepage for their current address.

Appendix B - Mother's and Father's Stone Clues

Gravestone	Year	Relationship	Headstone	Footstone
Insin Benjiamin Smith	1723	Military Officer		2 F-D-L
Insin Joseph Knight	1723	Military Officer	2 F-D-L	2 F-D-L
Abigail Sawyer	1722	Wife	1 F-D-L	
Samuel Sawyer	1723	Husband	2 F-D-L	
Mary Sawyer	1708	Mother	2 HEARTS	2 F-D-L
John Sawyer	1723	Son/name "John"	2 HEARTS	2 F-D-L
John Knight	1723	Name "John"	2 HEARTS	
John Brown	1724	Name "John"	2 HEARTS	
Issac Bayliy	1726	Not applicable (SEE: "Notes")		2 HEARTS

F-D-L = Fleur-de-lis

NOTES: Issac's hearts are the only other set used by Robert Mullicken, Sr. (They were carved on the footstone not the headstone like the others). They set Issac apart from other family members only. The Bayley's were another noted family in Second Parish where they are buried in Sawyers Hill Burying Ground.

Hearts were also used by Robert's three sons. However, their hearts span twelve years and show no particular pattern. They were used on gravestones in several towns and placed on both men and women's graves. Their hearts vary from single to pairs and were used in different arrangements.

Appendix C - Burying Grounds

> **NOTE:** Please consult Appendix "A" for a list of gravestones used in this study and the cemeteries they are located in. This is not a comprehensive list of all the cemeteries which contain stones by Hartshorn or the Mullickens.

Belleville, Newburyport, MA

This burying ground is on Storey Avenue/Route 113 which is a continuation (left at "Y") of High Street. It is across the street from Shaw's shopping center. The two oldest gravestones dated 1727 and 1732 were done by John Mullicken and are located in the section on Route 113 near the traffic light. Samuel Bartlett's gravestone was the one used in this study but Sarah Bartlett's interesting footstone contributed to the overall study.

Bradford Burying Ground: Bradford, MA

Bradford Burying Ground is located on Salem Street (off of Route 125). The old section begins where the hill descends in the back. In a row about half ways down the hill is Robert Mullicken, Jr.'s gravestone. At the bottom of the hill towards the side road are the graves of Robert Mullicken, Sr. and his son, John. In this back section, there are many examples of both the Mullicken family and Hartshorn carved gravestones.

Bridge Street Cemetery, West Newbury, MA

Bridge Street Cemetery is located on Bridge Street (off of Route 113). This cemetery contains a few examples of the Mullicken's stones.

Church Street Cemetery: Merrimac, MA

Church Street Cemetery is located on Church Street (off of Route 110). The gravestones carved by the Mullickens are located in northern end near the stone wall.

First Cemetery: Salisbury, MA

First Cemetery is located on Beach Road / Route 1A across from the Star of The Sea Church. It is a small cemetery which contains some examples of Hartshorn's stones.

First Parish Burying Ground: Newbury, MA

This burying ground is located on High Road/Route 1A across from the First Parish Church of Newbury near the upper green with the frog pond. The old graves are laid out in a three sided square that once surrounded the old meeting house. New graves now occupy the old building's space. The majority of the older stones are concentrated in the north side of the cemetery. In this section along the main path are located three of the Dummer graves (one is missing). This section can be accessed by the northern most gate. Also in this cemetery are the gravestones of Lunt, Brown, Knight, Greenleaf, Pierce and Stickney whose stones are included in this research. This cemetery contains the work of Hartshorn and the Mullickens.

Old Burying Ground, Ipswich, MA

It is located on High Street. The oldest section is the tier at road level. This cemetery houses the oldest surviving gravestone (1647). It also has examples of John Harthorn's work from the circa 1710-1719 time period.

Old Hill Burying Ground: Newburyport, MA

This burying ground is located on Greenleaf Street and Pond Street (off of High Street, Newburyport). It was started in 1730 and has two gravestones used in the project. They are Amos Beck and Richard Titcomb both located at the very top of the hill near a large above ground tomb.

Pentucket Burying Ground: Haverhill, MA

Pentucket is located at the intersection of Route 97/113/Water Street and Mill Street. Parking is available in the Linwood cemetery on Mill Street. Once you enter the Linwood Cemetery turn right and follow the road until you see a chain link fence. The fence divides the Pentucket from Linwood. This burying ground contains Hartshorn's earliest work and the combined gravestone his wife Joanna and his son John.

Riverview Cemetery: Groveland, MA

Riverview Cemetery is located on Main Street (Route 113). The entrance is marked by a large stone archway. The oldest section is on the left of the middle road just beyond the entrance. About in the middle of this section is Joseph Mullicken's gravestone.

Rowley Burying Ground: Rowley, MA

The old Rowley Burying Ground is located on Route 1A in the center of town across from the town green. This cemetery contains Hartshorn's gravestone for Sara Wicomb the lady with a crown. It is located in the old section near the center road on the left about a quarter of the way back from the main road (Rt. 1A) There are a few fairly well persevered gravestones here but a lot more of Hartshorn's work is in Ipswich down the road about five miles. Ipswich's burying ground is on the left where Route 1A branches off to the right to go into the downtown area of Ipswich.

Sawyers Hill Burying Ground: Newburyport, MA

To find this burying follow the signs to Maudsley State Park. It can be easily reached from Route 113 via Noble Road that separates Belleville and St. Mary's cemeteries, watch for the signs at end of road. Park in the state park's parking lot. Next to the parking lot on the same side are two houses, Sawyers Hill is located behind the houses. It can be accessed via the road that looks like a driveway between the houses or from the field behind the parking lot. The Sawyers are in the far back corner. Smith and Knight are in amongst other examples of Mullicken family carved gravestones located within the back quarter section.

Appendix D

The following illustrations are two drawings from the Stephen P. Hale Papers deposited at the Byfield Public Library. They come from a manuscript paged titled "Drawings made from rocks on the Newbury Poor Farm in South Byfield." The Newbury Poor Farm was the site of the Dummer family mansion house and farm (Watkins, 1969). The page contains three drawings (the third being the 1640 doorstone).

"From the House Cellar"

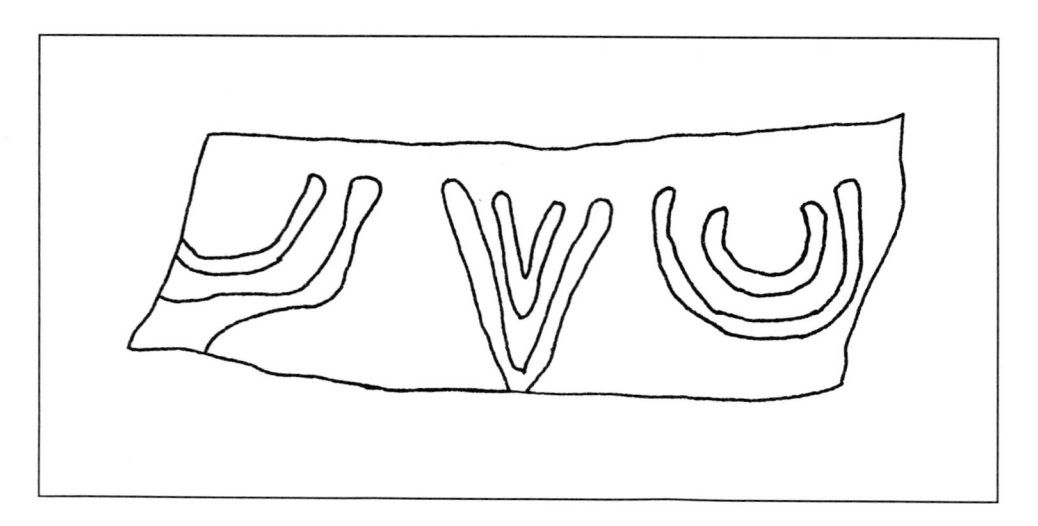

"Edge of rock in ----- under wall"

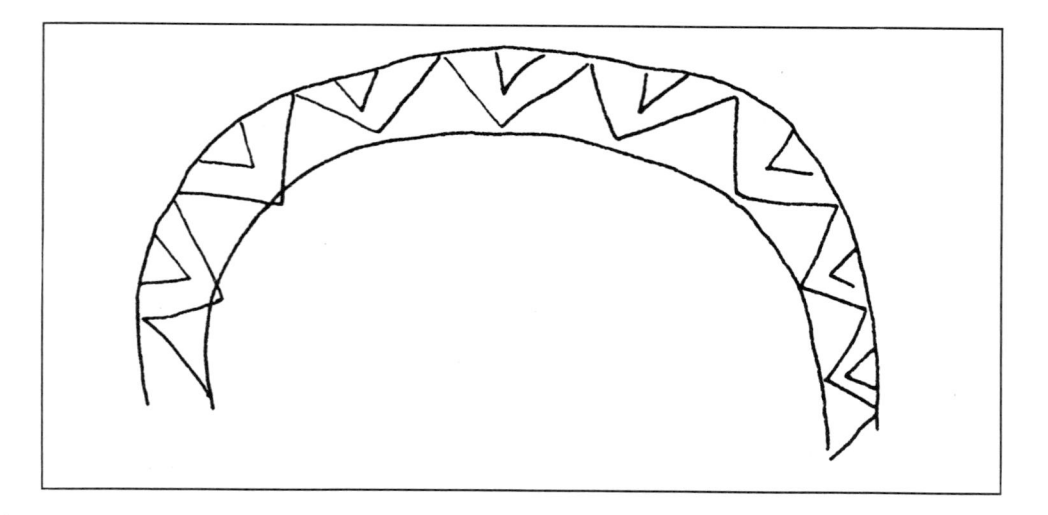

Bibliography

American Federation of Arts
1969 *American Naïve Painting of the 18th and 19th Centuries*. American Federation of Arts.

Beaudry, Mary C.
n. d. *"Above Vulgar Economy": Material Culture and Social Positioning among Newburyport's Merchant Elite*. Unpublished draft 11/26/95.

Benes, Peter
1986 A Particular Sense of Doom: Skeletal "Revivals" in Northern Essex County, Massachusetts 1737 - 1784. *Markers III*. 3: 71 - 92. Worcester, MA: Association for Gravestone Studies.
1973 Lt. John Hartshorn: Gravestone Maker of Haverhill and Norwich. *Essex Institute Historical Collections*. 109: 152 - 164. Salem, MA: Essex Institute.
1977 *The Masks of Orthodoxy*. Amherst, MA: The University of Massachusetts Press.

Berube, Margery S. (Editor)
1985 *The American Heritage Dictionary*. 2nd Ed. Boston, MA: Houghton Mifflin Co.

Bigelow, Francis H.
1917 *Historic Silver of the Colonies and its Makers*. New York, NY: Macmillan Co.

Bouchard, Betty J.
1991 *Our Silent Neighbors: A Study of Gravestones in the Olde Salem Area*. Salem, MA: T.B.S. Enterprises.

Boumphrey, Geoffrey (Editor)
1985 *The New Shell Guide to Britain*. Salem, NH: Salem House. Rev. Ed.

Britannica
1994 *The New Encyclopedia Britannica*. Vol. 8. Chicago: Encyclopedia Britannica, Inc.

Buel, Joy D., Buel, Richard, Jr.
1984 *The Way of Duty: A Woman and Her Family in Revolutionary America*. New York, NY: W. W. Norton & Co.

Byfield (Parish), Massachusetts
1953 Byfield Parish Records October 29, 1706 - March 2, 1762. *Essex Institute Historical Collections*. 89: 163-194. Salem, MA: Essex Institute. [Salem, MA: Newcomb & Gauss, Co. Printers.]

Clarke, Herman Frederick and Foote, Henry Wilder
1935 *Jeremiah Dummer, Colonial Craftsman and Merchant, 1645 - 1718*. Boston, MA: Houghton Mifflin Co. [Book in library of Brick House Museum, Wells, ME]

Coffin, Joshua
1845 *A Sketch of the History of Newbury, Newburyport, and West Newbury from 1635 to 1845*. Boston, MA: S. G. Drake

Court, A. N.
n. d. *Colourful England*. Jarrold - Norwich.

Crawford, Mary C.
1907 *Little Pilgrimages Among Old New England Inns*. Boston, MA: L. C. Page & Company.

Currier, John J.
1896 *Ould Newbury: Historical and Biographical Sketches.* Boston, MA: Damrell & Upham.
1902 *History of Newbury, Mass. 1635-1902.* Boston, MA: Damrell & Upham.

Deetz, James
1977 *In Small Things Forgotten.* New York, NY: Anchor Books.

Dummer, Joseph N.
1888 *A Brief History of Byfield.* Salem, MA: Observer and Job Print.

Earle, Alice M.
1901 *Stage Coach and Tavern Days.* New York, NY: Macmillan Co.

Essex County, Massachusetts
1912 *Records and Files of the Quarterly Courts of Essex County, Massachusetts.* Salem, MA: Essex Institute.
1916 *The Probate Records of Essex County Massachusetts.* Salem, MA: The Essex Institute.

Ewell, John L.
1904 *The Story of Byfield.* Boston, MA: George E. Littlefield.

Forbes, Harriet
1927 *Gravestones of Early New England.* Boston, MA: Houghton Mifflin Co.

Friar, Stephen (Editor)
1987 *A Dictionary of Heraldry.* New York, NY: Harmony Books.

Gage, Thomas
1840 *The History of Rowley.* Boston, MA: F. Andrews.

Hurd, D. Hamilton
1888 *History of Essex County, Massachusetts with Biographical Sketches of many of its Pioneers.* Philadelphia, PA: J. W. Lewis & Co.

Morison, Samuel Eliot
1981 [1930] *Builders of the Bay Colony.* Boston, MA: Northeastern University Press.

Hart, Roger
1970 *English Life in the Seventeenth Century.* New York, NY: G. P. Putman & Sons.

Hosmer, James K. (Editor)
1908 *Winthrop's Journal "History of New England" 1630-1649.* New York, NY: Charles Scribner's Sons. 2 volumes.

Hovey, Horace C.
1900 Symbolic Rocks of Newbury and Byfield, Mass. *Scientific American Supplement.* No. 1299: 20821 – 20822 (November 24, 1900).

Hurd, D. Hamilton
1888 *History of Essex County Massachusetts with Biographical Sketches of Many of its Pioneers and Prominent Men.* Philadelphia, PN: J. S. Lewis & Co.

Jewett, Amos E., & Jewett, Emily M.
1946 *Rowley, Massachusetts: "Mr. Ezechi Rogers Plantation," 1639-1850.* Rowley, MA: Jewett Family of America. (Salem, MA: Newcomb & Guass)

Marlowe, George Francis
1954 *Byroads of Old New England.* New York, NY: Exposition Press

Massachusetts Historical Society
1852-1871   Massachusetts Historical Society Collections, 4th Series. [Vols. I – X].

Newbury, Massachusetts
1911   *Vital Records of Newbury Massachusetts to the Year ending 1849.* Salem, MA: The Essex Institute.

Noble, John
1904   *Records of the Court of Assistants of the Colony of the Massachusetts Bay, 1630-1692.* Boston, MA: County of Suffolk.

Oswald, Barron
1903   *The Ancestor.* 6: 162. July 1903.

Phillips, James D.
1945   Governor Dummer's Family and School. *Essex Institute Historical Collections.* 81: 35 - 53. Salem, MA: Essex Institute. [Salem, MA: Newcomb & Gauss, Co. Printers.]

Sanborn, F. B.
1900   *The Hard Case of the Founder of Old Hampton.* Available at Lane Memorial Library, Hampton NH or online at http://www.hampton.lib.nh.us/hampton/biog/bachilerhardcase.htm

Sanborn, Victor C.
1917   *Stephen Bachiler: An Unforgiven Puritan.* New Hampshire Historical Society. Available at Lane Memorial Library, Hampton NH or online at http://www.hampton.lib.nh.us/hampton/biog/bachilerunforgiven.htm

Shurtleff, Nathaniel B. (Editor)
1853   *Records of the Governor and Company of the Massachusetts Bay Colony in New England.* Boston, MA: Press of William White.

Slater, James A., Tucker, Ralph L., Farber, Daniel
1978   The Colonial Gravestones Carvings of John Hartshorn. *Puritan Gravestone Art 11.* pp. 79 - 146. Dublin Seminar for New England Folklife. Annual Proceedings 1978. Boston, MA: Boston University. [Ed. Peter Benes]

Sloane, Eric
1956   *Eric Sloane's America.* New York, NY: Promontory Press.

Stier, Margaret M.
1983   'Wonderfully Lettered and Carved': The Gravestones of the Risley Family, 1786-1835. *Dartmouth College Library Bulletin.* Vol. XXIII no. 2, April 183, pp. 58-88 Hanover, NH : Dartmouth College Libraries.

Stillinger, Elizabeth
1972   *The Antiques Guide to Decorative Arts in America 1600 - 1875.* New York, NY: E. P. Dutton & Co., Inc.

Suffolk County, MA
1885   *Suffolk Deeds.* Boston, Rockwell & church, City Printers.

Tepper, Michael (Editor)
1978   *Passengers to America: A Consolidation of Ship Passenger Lists from the New England Historical and Genealogical Register.* Baltimore, MD: Genealogical Publishing Co., Inc.

Tucker, Ralph L.
1989   Overview of Essex County Gravestone Carvers. Paper presented at conference of the Association of Gravestone Studies.
1992   The Mullicken Family Gravestone Carvers of Bradford, Massachusetts: 1663 - 1768. *Markers IX*. 9: 23 - 55. Worcester, MA: Association for Gravestone Studies.
1994   Merrimac Valley Style Gravestones: The Leighton and Worster Families. *Markers XI*. 11: 143-167. Worcester, MA: Association for Gravestone Studies.

Watkins, Lura W.
1963   The Byfield Stones - Our Earliest American Sculpture*? Antiques Magazine*. Oct 1963: 420 - 423.
1969   The Dummer Family and the Byfield Carvings. *Essex Institute Historical Collections*. 105: 3 - 30. Salem, MA: Essex Institute. [Salem, MA: Newcomb & Gauss, Printers.]

Weymouth, D. G.
n.d.   *Research of D. G. Weymouth.*
         http://www.weymouthtech.com/Genealogy/ps66/ps66_207.htm

Wood, Fredric J.
1919   *The Turnpikes of New England: And the Evolution of the Same Through England, Virginia, and Maryland.* Boston, MA: Marshall Jones Company.

Zieber, Eugene
1977   *Heraldry in America.* Baltimore, MD: Genealogy Publishing Co., Inc.